TEACHING THE EDUCABLE MENTALLY RETARDED

— Practical Methods —

1. *(Frontispiece)* Student teacher and pupil, Mrs. Garton's group, Illinois State Normal University, Normal, Illinois.

TEACHING THE EDUCABLE MENTALLY RETARDED

— Practical Methods —

By

MALINDA DEAN GARTON, A.M.

Assistant Professor and Supervising Teacher
Intermediate Educable Mentally Retarded
Thomas J. Metcalf School
Illinois State Normal University
Normal, Illinois

CHARLES C THOMAS • PUBLISHER
Springfield • Illinois • U.S.A.

CHARLES C THOMAS • PUBLISHER
BANNERSTONE HOUSE
301-327 East Lawrence Avenue, Springfield, Illinois, U.S.A.

Library of Congress Catalog Card Number 60-15848

Printed in the United States of America

To my sons, Norman Lee and Martin William, from whom I have learned much about youth; and to my grandchildren, from whom I am still learning—Richard Dean, Ina Malinda, Roland Lee, Ray Lester, and Lilinda Fay.

PREFACE

Practical Methods for Teaching the Educable Mentally Retarded is restricted in its scope to problems directly related with teaching the educable mentally retarded. This non-technical book consists of information, suggestions, examples, and methods of teaching from the readiness stage to the pre-vocational areas.

The content of this book includes detailed information which the teacher, parent, or other worker should know in order to help the mentally retarded. The etiology and psychology of these children are not included; but characteristics, objectives in education, curriculum suggestions, and methods for carrying out the suggestions are described. The material is presented in an informal, condensed style.

The bibliography contains references of interest to those who care for the scientific, personal anecdote or further information concerning the mentally retarded.

This book is written for those who work with the retarded in the belief that these experiences, suggestions, examples, and methods will give them a better understanding of the educable mentally retarded child. It presents practical plans for helping the retarded child retain and use the material to which he is introduced during his school tenure.

The methods should guide the inexperienced teacher in planning and carrying out her daily schedule. They are also aids for the experienced teacher who finds satisfaction in new plans and materials. They should inspire the regular class teacher to include plans for the mentally retarded child in her group so that he, too, may achieve some success.

MALINDA DEAN GARTON

Danvers, Illinois

ACKNOWLEDGMENTS

I wish to express my appreciation to all those who have assisted in any way in the preparation of the book, including the following:

Miss A. Grace Hiler, Assistant Professor of English, University High School, Illinois State Normal University, for her editorial assistance, invaluable criticism, and encouragement during the final preparation of the manuscript;

Mrs. Vera Moon, Special Teacher of Dependent and Delinquent Children, Gift Avenue School, Peoria, Illinois, who first encouraged the writing of this book and gave suggestions concerning its scope;

Miss Dorothy M. McEvoy, Assistant Professor and Teacher of the Deaf, Metcalf School, Illinois State Normal University, who gave helpful advice and encouragement;

Miss Lillie Mae Rickman, Assistant Professor and Associate Principal of Metcalf School, Illinois State Normal University, for understanding consideration during the final preparation of the manuscript;

Nelson R. Smith, Assistant Professor and Official Photographer, Illinois State Normal University, and his helpers for their patience and skill in capturing representative poses of the children in the classroom and other illustrative materials for the book;

Wilbur Ludwig, commercial artist, Bloomington, Illinois, for his patience and care in preparing the ink illustrations;

Miss Gloria Reyes, Jose Abad Santos Memorial School, Philippine Women's University, Manila, P.I., for introducing the "Tinikling" dance to the children;

Silver Burdett Company, Morristown, N. J., for permission to use directions for the "Tinikling" from *The Philippine Progressive Music Series,* Primary Grades, copyright 1948;

My student teachers from 1950 through 1960, who helped make

my teaching an even more rewarding experience, with special mention to D. Wayne Ruble, Kay Eich Wilhelmi and Juanita Lynn;

Also to Kay Lindenbaum Crane, Emmajo Luke McPherson, Eileen Joyce Seymour, James Seay, Carolyn Jones Dobbins, Joan Lane, Carol Touzinsky, Barbara Thiessen, Dorothy Hafstrom, and Carol Brubaker Kaliher for bulletin board materials and arithmetic devices;

Also Karen Reedy, Dianne Thiessen, Alice Moxey, Jacqueline Dudnick, Virginia Huisinga, and Colleen Mauterer for reading parts of the manuscript and giving helpful suggestions.

MALINDA DEAN GARTON

CONTENTS

Page

Preface vii
Acknowledgments ix

Chapter

1. OBJECTIVES FOR THE EDUCABLE MENTALLY RETARDED 3
   The Purpose of the Program 3
   The Four General Objectives 4
   Physical and Mental Health 5
   Value of Praise and Love 5
   Summary 6

2. CHARACTERISTICS OF THE EDUCABLE MENTALLY RETARDED 7
   Definition of Educable Mentally Retarded 7
   Characteristics of the Educable Mentally Retarded 7
   What Is the Future of the Educable Mentally Retarded 11
   Summary 11

3. THE CURRICULUM 12
   Groups Under the Special Curriculum 12
   Multiple Handicaps 13
   Curriculum 14
   The Modified Core Curriculum 15
   Building a Unit of Work 17
   The Unit Outline 19
   Explanation of Unit Outline 20
   Integration with Other Areas 26
   Reading in the Core Curriculum 28
   Summary 31

Chapter *Page*

4. TEACHING TECHNIQUES AND GENERAL EXPERIENCES 33
   The Unit as a Complete Experience 33
   Methods for Teaching the Unit and the Basic Skills 33
   Audio-visual Aids in the Unit 34
   Experience Charts 34
   Flash Cards for Word Drill 34
   Activities for Drill 34
   To Improve Sight Vocabulary 35
   Visual Discrimination 38
   Visual and Auditory Discrimination 39
   Confusion Words and Letters 39
   Speech Defects 39
   Markers for Reading 39
   Oral Reading 39
   Comprehension 40
   Exercises for Comprehension 40
   General Experiences 41
   Discipline for the Mentally Retarded 62
   Teacher-Parent Relationships 63
   Summary 66

5. UNITS OF WORK 67
   Summer Fun 67
   Bibliography 78
   The Weather 84
   Clouds 89

6. WRITING 93
   The Objectives in Teaching Writing 93
   Importance of Establishing Correct Habits 93
   Value of Writing One's Name 93
   Introduction of Cursive Writing 94
   Manuscript Writing 95
   Presentation of the First Manuscript Writing Lesson 97
   Tracing in Clay 99

Chapter | Page

Kinesthetic Training 101
Consonants 102
Practice on Endings 103
Length of Writing Period 103
Use of Alphabet Charts 103
Summary 103

7. SPELLING 104
Summary 107

8. MUSIC 108
A Folk Dance 111
Summary 112

9. ART 113
Purpose of the Art Program 113
Summary 126

10. AUDIO-VISUAL AND OTHER SENSORY TRAINING 127
Purpose of Using Audiovisual and Sensory Materials 127
Selection of Audio-visual Materials 127
Activities for Training the Senses 131
Summary 135

11. THE BULLETIN BOARD 136
Materials and Their Use 136
Supplementary Materials 138
Summary 138

12. THE SOCIOGRAM 139
The Purpose of the Sociogram 139
Procedure 139
Questions for a Sociogram 142
Summary 143

Chapter *Page*

13. ARITHMETIC 144
    Arithmetic for the Educable Mentally Retarded 144
    Progress Chart and Check List 149
    Teaching Number Concepts 153
    Other Topics 190
    Summary 207

Bibliography 209

Index 223

TEACHING THE EDUCABLE MENTALLY RETARDED

— Practical Methods —

I

OBJECTIVES FOR THE EDUCABLE MENTALLY RETARDED

THE PURPOSE OF THE PROGRAM

THE overall aim in a school program for educable mentally retarded children is to contribute to their ultimate development into self-sufficient citizens. To help accomplish this general aim, situations must be developed to provide the children with problems and a need to solve the problems. The teacher must help the children establish good work habits which will include training with experiences designed to promote emotional stability and self-confidence. The training should also aid the pupils to realize their abilities as well as their limitations.

With this training and an interest created in personalized problems, self-centered lives may be guided into concern for others. This knowledge and concern should be used by the teacher to develop attitudes, habits, and abilities that will assist the mentally retarded to succeed in vocational training programs.

These mentally retarded children should also become acquainted with our cultural and spiritual heritage, as well as with our historical background. They must be stimulated to a realization that this wonderful country of ours grew out of problems concerned with the human values and the personal rights of boys and girls, men and women.

Each new generation of children must be made aware of these values. They must be given a sense of belonging to this country and of being responsible for its continued growth and maintenance; otherwise, they may never become responsible citizens.

It is easy to understand how mentally retarded children become frustrated in school and why they have a negative attitude toward school and life in general. It is the teacher's duty to kindle in these children a desire to achieve self-sufficiency, to help them feel secure, and to give them a sense of being a part of our society. These children will respond to the teacher's efforts when they are relieved of pressure to accomplish impossible tasks in competition with children of far superior mental ability.

Major objectives for the education of all children have been outlined by the Educational Policies Commission. These four major goals are of value in preparing a program for the educable mentally retarded. The four general objectives should be modified and interpreted in relation to the needs and abilities of these children.

THE FOUR GENERAL OBJECTIVES

Self-realization. The mentally retarded child may achieve self-realization in so far as he is capable. A child may be slow in achieving academically, but he can learn to understand his abilities and disabilities. Through the development of the capacities he does possess, he will attain satisfaction academically, physically, and vocationally.

Social Competence. The educable mentally retarded child can learn how to take care of his personal hygiene and how to appear well groomed in order to be socially acceptable. He can learn how to behave adequately at social gatherings and in other public places. He can be trained to know how to meet ordinary situations in life. The teacher should strive to instill the ideals, attitudes, and emotional control necessary for social adjustment. She should try to help this child cultivate an interest in life about him—good friends, nature, sports, art, music, politics, and religion.

Economic Efficiency. The educable mentally retarded child can be trained to complete a job, to learn some skills, and to develop good work habits, good attitudes, and a pleasing personality. He can be taught the value of money and of planning, through establishing habits of thrift. He should learn where to go for counseling concerning family affairs. He should learn the value of securing legal and medical advice from professional sources.

The educable mentally retarded child must be adequately trained to know how to apply for a job, and to know what he must do to keep the job so that he may become economically self-sufficient.

Civic Responsibility. The teacher should help the educable mentally retarded child to prepare to assume civic responsibility. He should learn something about the laws of the town, the state, and the nation in which he lives. He should respect property, both public and private. He should develop the desire to be of service to his fellow man, to know how to vote, to know what he is voting about, and then to go and cast his ballot.

Interpretation of Curriculum. To accomplish the above four general objectives of education, the curriculum for the educable mentally retarded must be adaptable to each group's changing needs; it must be practical to encourage the learnings necessary to meet life's demands.

PHYSICAL AND MENTAL HEALTH

The success of a program for the educable mentally retarded depends partly upon the physical condition of the child, which has an important influence upon his emotional stability. A child in poor health is easily discouraged, depressed, or angered.

A healthy child has a better chance to make friends, to have a vocation, and, eventually, to become a respected member of a community. Better emotional health and social adjustment may be aided through the development of special health instruction courses and through proper and appropriate physical education classes. Many opportunities for personality growth should be provided through the areas of music, art, crafts, shop, dramatization, play therapy, and homemaking.

VALUE OF PRAISE AND LOVE

Each child should have praise and love given to him daily by his teacher. He should be made to feel that what he has accomplished is important to his teacher. After a while the child will begin to feel satisfied with himself. When he is freed from the strain of apprehension of failure and rejection, he will likely succeed in some area to compensate for former failures.

SUMMARY

It seems obvious that the teacher is responsible for providing helpful, happy, healthful, successful experiences for the educable mentally retarded. The teacher's aim through the use of these activities is to assist the development of self-realization, social competence, economic efficiency, and civic responsibility in each child to the best of his ability.

2

CHARACTERISTICS OF THE EDUCABLE MENTALLY RETARDED

These questions are often asked: What do you mean by an educable mentally retarded child? What are some of his predominant characteristics? What of this person's future?

DEFINITION OF EDUCABLE MENTALLY RETARDED

An educable mentally retarded child is defined by the Illinois Commission for Handicapped Children as "any child whose rate of mental development, as measured by individual psychological examinations, has been retarded from birth or early age, but who requires and may expect to benefit from special education facilities designed to make him economically useful and socially adjusted."

Too often we think of the educable mentally retarded child as just slightly different from the normal child. We should be aware of his special characteristics and behavioral patterns in order to find him and help him. Left without special help, he becomes lost and frustrated in competition with the usual children in school, work, or play.

CHARACTERISTICS OF THE EDUCABLE MENTALLY RETARDED

Sensitivity to Surroundings. The retarded child is usually quite sensitive to either hostile or friendly surroundings. He seems instinctively to know when the teacher accepts him, when the visitor is friendly, or when the visitor is merely tolerating him. Teachers, parents, and visitors should realize that this child must be loved for what he can do, instead of being rejected for what he is unable to do. Acceptance is important for the preservation of the child's dignity and the achievement of self-realization.

Without acceptance by the adults in his life, the child will show resentment in tantrums, sulking, inattention, hyperactivity, defacing property, destroying work papers, crying, or arguing. Special training and experience are necessary to understand how to approach the child. The teacher or worker must know when to be firm, when to ignore an act, and when to move to another activity to forestall unpleasant situations.

Slow Reaction Time. Most mentally retarded children have a better manual dexterity than mental performance, but it still is not in the normal range of ability. Even in a manual program, mentally retarded children are called stubborn, lazy, and disobedient, because they have a slow reaction time.

These children are unable to become interested in a new activity without first adjusting to the idea. The teacher should give them time to put away their materials from the previous activity. If it has been an art period, she should allow them time to admire their products and to clear away the crayons, papers, or paints. She should provide for a brief rest period before suggesting a new activity. Too much haste by the instructor may bring on a temper tantrum or other objectionable behavior that could have been avoided.

Short Attention Span. The mentally retarded child may listen to or look at any thing for brief periods. The teacher will discover that the child's attention may wander from an enjoyable activity; yet he will not wish to relinquish the activity.

The less interest the child has in an activity, the more easily he becomes distracted. Therefore, all of the material used for teaching the mentally retarded must be at the child's level of interest and comprehension; the activities must be geared to his short attention span, and the material must be within his ability to complete with a reasonable feeling of satisfaction.

Poor Transfer of Learning. The mentally retarded child has a poor ability to transfer learning from one situation to another. For this reason, the teacher should take nothing for granted.

Each situation is a new and difficult experience for this child. The teacher should remember that even though the child knows how to spell *can,* she should not expect him to spell *pan.* Even though he knows the sound of the beginning consonant *p* and the ending *an,* he needs much help in associating and blending the sounds into a word.

Lack of Initiative for Planning. Mentally retarded children are the followers of the world. They are easily led into gangs and subsequently into delinquency, or they are led into vocational training to become helpers in our society.

Limited Imagination. The educable mentally retarded tend to be practical. They seem to be unable to do work requiring originality, imagination, and creativeness. They are able to imitate and to vary the finished product with fanciful or playful additions. The teacher or pupils are rarely aware of the amount of teacher structuring that has gone into any finished product.

The educable mentally retarded have some facility at *fancy,* which Fernald defines as being a mental image found upon capricious or whimsical association or resemblence.

Limited Use of Concepts. The educable mentally retarded are seldom able to apply separate qualities to the solution of problems. Abstract terms, such as *four, multiply, sympathy,* are difficult to understand. In developing concepts, the teacher should not only be explicit but use simple language. She should use a variety of experiences and demonstrations to ensure comprehension and retention.

Small Vocabulary. A serious defect of mentally retarded children is their inability to communicate. They do not understand most of the words used in ordinary conversation. Prepositions are especially baffling. Children who do not respond readily to a direction may not understand the meaning of a term used, such as *over, under, between,* or *below.*

Inability to Evaluate Efforts. The mentally retarded have little ability to evaluate their own efforts. The teacher should give deserved praise to strengthen confidence in their ability to perform designated tasks. Conversely, she should point out defects in workmanship and give help to develop better skills.

Narrow Range of Interest. Frequently the children of this group, because of poor ability to observe and make use of previous experiences, are lacking in a knowledge of common events and places, as well as in good manners, morals and ethical conduct. The teacher should provide for special instruction and activities to promote the attainment of these qualities.

Normal Physical Maturation. The physical maturation of the mentally retarded approximates that of the normal child. The emotional needs and pressures of both groups of children are similar. Because the retarded child has a limited vocabulary for verbal expression, his feelings become crowded with repressions and frustrations. Consequently, his emotional problems are often greater than those of the normal child.

Difficulty in Recognizing Boundaries. The mentally retarded child usually does not recognize boundaries. This characteristic applies to his dealings with such things as physical and moral issues or property rights. The boundary of the child's playground may be outlined with shrubbery; yet he is unable to realize that the property outside of that boundary belongs to someone else.

This child may walk about the classroom to get a drink and start back to his seat. On his way he may see a pencil on a desk that he needs for his seat work. He picks it up and carries it to his desk, where he uses it to work his problems. Afterwards, although he no longer needs it, he does not return it to the owner.

The educable mentally retarded child does not readily recognize the shapes of objects, such as circles, squares, or oblongs. He has difficulty in associating the name and the shape of the object. This same difficulty appears when he is asked to identify his cap, gloves, or a painting in an unfamiliar setting. However, when he does recognize his belongings, he is usually fiercely possessive.

Difficulty in Distinguishing Right from Wrong. The inability to distinguish right from wrong frequently causes the mentally retarded to become involved in actions leading to the juvenile court. The teacher must realize that, because these children are usually unable to generalize, they should be taught definitely that certain actions are *right* or *wrong*. The teacher needs to be alert to grasp every opportunity to impress upon the mentally retarded the highest social and moral values.

Limited Sense of Humor. Mentally retarded children have a crude sense of humor. They enjoy practical jokes and may laugh at a serious accident. Jokes that the ordinary child would consider funny do not rate a smile. Witty remarks are lost when directed to them as the words convey no meaning.

Ability to Be Loyal. Once the mentally retarded person has accepted the teacher or employer, he has a strong sense of loyalty and attachment for that person. If he is treated with fairness and consideration, he will remain with that person as long as he is allowed to do so.

Ability to Acquire Habits. The educable mentally retarded are strongly bound by habits. The teacher should be careful to prepare all activities in such a manner that the material is presented the first time in the way she wishes the project to be completed. It is difficult to change the procedure of teaching these children to do anything once a habit has been formed.

WHAT IS THE FUTURE OF THE EDUCABLE MENTALLY RETARDED

These boys and girls will develop into homemakers, parents, voters, taxpayers, homeowners, or renters. At the age of twenty-one they become citizens of our country. How useful their citizenship becomes to our town, state, and nation depends largely upon the training they receive during their formative years. Their employment possibility is based upon emotional stability and the ability to take orders and to carry out directions.

SUMMARY

The teacher should realize that the educable mentally retarded have many characteristics that should be considered when she plans activities for them. Because they observe few details of any object or incident, they fail to understand a situation, to recognize an object, or to find a solution to a problem. They are unable to interpret others' actions or to speculate on the results of their own actions. Good habits must be formed through the teacher's presentation of many lessons and dramatizations demonstrating right from wrong.

3

THE CURRICULUM

GROUPS UNDER THE SPECIAL CURRICULUM

THE eligibility of children for the special services of a room for the educable mentally retarded is determined by tests and psychological examinations. These children are usually separated into four groups according to their chronological age and their physical and social maturity.

The Primary Group. The primary group of children are usually within the chronological age bracket of six to ten years. They are retained in the primary group for three to four years, depending upon their entrance age and maturity.

Since the mental age of these primary children is generally under the age acceptable for academic work, the program here is largely devoted to helping them become socially adjusted and to acquiring academic readiness.

The Intermediate Group. The intermediate group of mentally retarded children is usually within the chronological age range of nine or ten to thirteen years. These children remain with the same teacher for three or four years, depending upon their entrance age and maturity.

They should be introduced to a curriculum designed to develop academic skills; to continue strengthening abilities in the areas of music, art, and health; and to begin new experiences in the areas of homemaking and industrial arts.

The Junior High School Group. The junior high school group of educable mentally retarded children is usually within the chronological age range of thirteen to sixteen years. They remain with their teacher for three or four years. The academic and socializing program is continued with this older group. It is augmented by beginning preparation for economic security through pre-vocational training.

The High School Group. The young people in the high school group of educable mentally retarded are usually within the chronological ages of fifteen to eighteen years.

As these young people are promoted to high school groups, their experience and maturity, plus the habits they have been carefully taught, result in better cooperation with supervisors and the start of inner control in preparation for community living. These acquired and superimposed habits will carry the individual through favorable and familiar situations. Teachers should realize, however, and prospective employers should be aware of, the probability of relapse under tension and frustration.

Since the retarded have poor judgment, they are unable to project and deduce the possible results of their actions. Consequently, they are unable to meet the demands of new situations. It is by constant drill on correct habit formation in both action and response that a more secure and responsible individual may be produced.

As these young people leave the school situation, they should go into work for which they have been partially prepared by their school experiences, which should include on-the-job training.

MULTIPLE HANDICAPS

The teacher of any group of mentally retarded children should be alert for the child in the room who is not responding to the program. The child may not be conforming to the expected pattern of the educable mentally retarded because of some physical or emotional disturbance. His non-conformity calls for a careful survey of his case history. A consultation or staffing may be necessary between the teacher, the parents, the school nurse, the child's doctor, the principal, the psychologist, and any other person closely associated with the child's life. The child may need special medication, therapy, or even surgery. He may be a child with a multiple handicap.

CURRICULUM

Scope and Content. The curriuculum for the educable mentally retarded must be practical. It should be constructed to suit the child's present and future needs. The scope and content of the curriculum should be determined by his interests and his ability to assimilate it and use it in everyday life.

The curriculum, which includes activities in academic and non-academic fields, should be considered as all of the child's experiences during his day at school. All of these activities should be so arranged and simplified that the educable mentally retarded child will be able to benefit from them. Many of the activities may be integrated within a unit of study; however, the basic skills should have special emphasis.

The teacher, the parent, the welfare worker, the school nurse, and the special area teachers need to work closely together to assist the child in maintaining good mental and physical health.

The teacher must first win the respect of the child and gain his confidence by always being fair and keeping promises. *The mentally retarded child does not take disappointments lightly.*

Areas for Lesson Material. The areas for academic lesson materials should be social situations, social science problems, and health and safety problems. Social experiences help the mentally

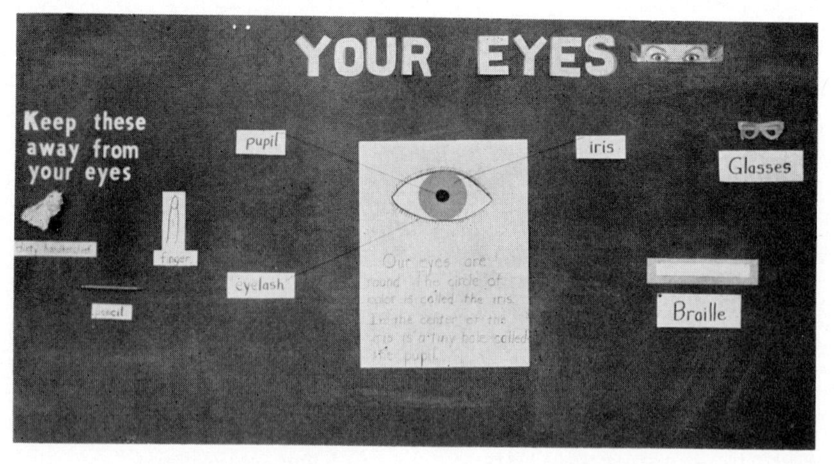

2. Bulletin board for a health unit on the care of the eyes.

retarded pupils to appreciate the contributions that others make to our society and to understand that they in turn have individual responsibilities toward others.

THE MODIFIED CORE CURRICULUM

The modified core curriculum as described in this chapter refers to studies dealing with human relationships structured around centers of interest in which the basic subjects are integrated. This plan allows for an overall understanding of some topic, with successful practice on many basic skills. As the areas are explored, the study assumes a lifelike aspect which provides motivation to the pupil for acquiring greater proficiency academically, manually, socially, and economically.

Purpose of the Modified Core Curriculum. The core unit of study provides a practical plan for teaching the educable mentally retarded children. This plan has proved successful in holding interest throughout a series of experiences and activities. It is also useful for motivating the retention of information and basic skills and for teaching other concepts and attitudes which lead to the final objective of producing a self-sufficient adult.

Place of the Core Unit in the Curriculum of the Educable Mentally Retarded. The core unit may be planned for the group by selecting a topic of interest in the area of human relationships as represented in the social studies or science fields, and by grouping materials, activities, and experiences around it from many areas, thus producing a coherent and cohesive unit of study. Such a study could be confined to one segment of a school day or enlarged to occupy all of the school day.

This type of integration should have some place on the daily schedule, even if it is only in a limited segment of time. The children are able to appreciate and understand lessons integrating reading, spelling, writing, social studies, arithmetic, nutrition, health, and safety. The chronological and mental ages, intelligence quotient, maturity, environment, and interests, as well as the ability to profit from activities and experiences, should be considered in planning all units of work for educable mentally retarded children.

Since each group of mentally retarded children will usually have a wide spread of ability in all areas, the teacher will find it expedient to plan work at more than one level. The youngest and the most immature pupils should have some special activities that are interesting and at which they may be successful; conversely, the older children and those with greater ability should have more challenging materials. Although the group may work together on many parts of the unit, they may be separated into small groups for the presentation of basic skills or explanations suited to their requirements.

Sources of Subjects for Units. Educators seem agreed that materials for the educable mentally retarded should spring from realistic situations. After deciding upon this situation, the teacher must prepare much of the material, since there are few available texts with the interest level and simple vocabulary these children require.

The teacher must provide the content or subject matter and the background material. She must prepare the details for presentation and for the integration of other areas of study or work. She

3. Bulletin board for a study of the community.

must plan for all of the activities and experiences in connection with the unit. She must prepare worksheets at several levels of ability to reinforce oral and demonstration teaching. The teacher must coordinate the preparation and presentation of all of these items and carry them through to completion.

As the teacher plans and develops the unit, she must keep in mind the necessity for intensive drill on basic skills and for adequate time to explain every detail. She must remember that the usual child picks up by observation many of the correct social behaviors of our culture, but the educable mentally retarded child does not observe these behaviors unless they are specifically pointed out to him. He will not know the common rules of courtesy and decency unless they are especially taught to him.

The teacher is responsible for building into the units materials and activities that will train the child to have attitudes and habits that are socially acceptable. These may include cleanliness, neatness, courtesy, promptness, honesty, and a respect for property both public and private.

BUILDING A UNIT OF WORK

Building a unit of work for the educable mentally retarded is an absorbing task that holds interest and rewards for the teacher, as well as for the pupils.

Types of Units. There are many types of units, among which are the following: Resource; Drill; Topic; Experience; Project; Activity; Block of Time, or Core.

Definition of a Unit. A unit is an organization of experiences and information around some topic of study.

The unit may be one simple, well-rounded endeavor to present a single problem, or it may outline a subject that covers a topic presenting many facets and requiring months of study to complete. Other interesting units may develop spontaneously from either the simple or the complex topics, some of which lend themselves more favorably to broad integration than do others. In adapting the use of the core curriculum to the requirements of the educable mentally retarded, it is not necessary to cover the entire range of civic and human activities or to include every possible opportunity to introduce a basic skill in reading, writing, or arithmetic. If the work is made too complex, the knowledge and the skills may be lost to these children. However, by keeping the structure of the unit simple, the overlapping of the learning areas has a decided advantage, since it helps to fix the information and skills for future use.

Selection of a Subject for a Unit. The selection of a topic for study, as well as the wording of the title, is important. If the title of the unit has appeal to the eye and ear, the children will be more interested. The subject should be introduced tentatively by questioning the children. The teacher should list the suggestions as they are made. She should be flexible and ready to consider a new topic if one is listed that has possibilities for development along the lines of the children's needs. If the children feel that they have selected the topic, they may have better motivation to pursue it.

In working with the educable mentally retarded, the teacher must encourage them to believe in themselves and in their suggestions. However, she must have an overall plan for them. When time permits, they should be included in the unit planning, which must be firmly directed, or the original purpose of the unit will never be attained. Later, after they have learned some of the background material about a subject, they often have good ideas for activities, especially for dramatizations.

If the teacher has a definite unit in view, she may introduce the problem by reading or telling a story; by asking questions; by showing pictures, films, film-strips, and materials that may be discussed; or by taking a field trip to make a preliminary survey to arouse interest.

The children's interest may be maintained throughout the development of the unit by keeping the content and the materials simple, direct, interesting, and dynamic. It is literally true that the teacher is competing with the movies and with television for the groups' attention and interest. Therefore, she should take a lesson from their methods of approach. She must resort to dramatization.

There are many heroes and incidents in our country's history that may be taught with as vivid dramatization as any fictional incident of the video screen. These true incidents provide excellent material for units of study to assist in character and attitude development.

The educable mentally retarded children enjoy the stories of Washington's boyhood on a farm and his struggles in the wilderness fighting the French and Indians. In the same way, they never seem to tire of stories about Lincoln. They understand and appreciate his hardships and mishaps.

Other sources for subject matter are space and the elements. Lessons concerning health and safety should be consistently taught throughout the year. These topics may be integrated into almost any unit of study.

THE UNIT OUTLINE

A unit should have some form or outline so that everything pertinent to the topic may be included. There are various forms that may be modified to suit a particular topic or condition. The one given here is a suggestion.

Plan for a Modified Core Unit

I. The Problem
II. General statement of the purpose of the unit
III. Objectives
IV. Motivation
V. Content
VI. Procedure
  A. Initiating
  B. Developing
  C. Culminating activities
VII. Materials
VIII. Evaluation
IX. Bibliography
  A. Books
  B. Magazines
  C. Other printed materials

D. Audio-Visual
   1. Films, Film-strips
   2. Pictures
   3. Other sensory materials
E. Music
   1. Songs
   2. Rhythms
   3. Recordings
F. Art
G. Crafts
H. Homemaking and Industrial Arts

The Daily Lesson Plan. A special plan must be made for each day's lesson. This must be thoroughly prepared if the lesson is to accomplish any purpose. The topic of the core units, as well as the purpose and general objectives, should always be kept in mind. In each lesson as much integration of the basic skills should be used as is possible without creating absurd and unnatural situations. This plan should include the objectives, materials, procedure, and a record of the outcomes with suggestions for the next lesson.

EXPLANATION OF UNIT OUTLINE

Unit Topic. The unit topic is the title of the study which will probe into, and combine, several areas of subject matter and integrate some of the basic skills.

Purpose of the Unit. The purpose or aim of the unit should be stated in one or two specific sentences. These statements should answer the question: Why is this unit being taught?

Objectives. The objectives for teaching the unit should be listed in detail so that they may be used as the source for the experiences and activities carried on throughout the development of the unit.

Motivation. To insure enthusiastic reception and retention of the material provided in the unit, the instructor must provide a sound motivation to create spontaneous interest. Motivation means to incite, to induce, to stimulate through appeal to associated interests or by special devices. It is of prime importance

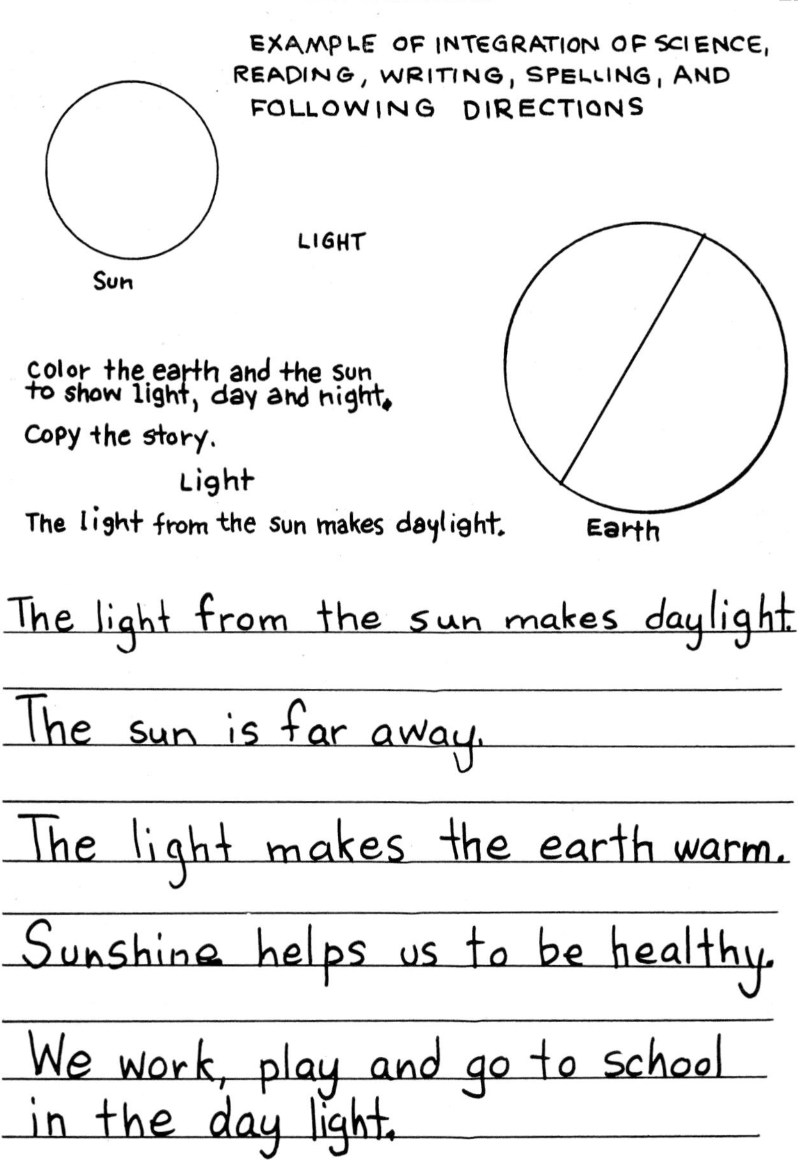

4. Worksheet—an example of integration of basic skills.

that the teacher stimulate a desire to read so that she can take advantage of the child's complete potential ability in all of the other learning processes.

The motivation for the unit as a whole must be directed toward the pupils' interests or greatest needs. For the older pupils a unit on communication might develop out of the pupils' need to know how to use the telephone, how to fill out an application for a job, or how to write the answers to the questions on tests for their drivers' licenses.

Other ways to motivate enthusiasm are through personal conferences and interest inventories. Topics for units of study may also arise out of such interests as hobbies, pets, future plans, a part-time job, wages, fishing, airplanes, space travel, a trip to the museum, dolls, a play house, or a game.

The Content. The content of the unit must be practical and demonstrable. The educable mentally retarded learn by seeing, handling, and doing. Reading, writing, and spelling are based on the subject of the unit. The material is prepared by the teacher to avoid wasted effort, frustration, and loss of interest on the part of the pupils.

The materials should be within the pupils' comprehension and ability to use with security and satisfaction. Each experience should be followed by a class discussion. A story of some kind should be developed in the same manner that experience charts are created in the primary room. The teacher should use the story as a basis for preparing worksheets for the next day's lesson.

These worksheets may be made in somewhat the same form as the lessons in workbooks that accompany commercially prepared reading, science, or social study books. However, the worksheets for the educable mentally retarded are prepared on levels commensurate with the pupils' abilities. These questions, exercises in matching or filling in blanks, should provide for the determining of comprehension, sight vocabulary recognition, sequence of ideas, and word meanings.

This worksheet form has been found most practical when it has been made at three levels of ability, because usually the children in the educable mentally retarded room can be separated into three groups. Worksheets for the readiness and primer group

EXAMPLE OF COMPREHENSIVE AND VOCABULARY TEST WITH SPELLING AND WRITING.

THE EARTH

FILL IN THE BLANKS WITH THESE WORDS:
WE, LIVE, ON, EARTH, ROUND

THE EARTH IS ______.
WE ______ ON THE EARTH.
THE ______ IS ROUND.
WE LIVE ______ THE EARTH.

FILL IN THE BLANKS WITH THESE WORDS: SHINES, MAKES, PLANTS, GROW, SUNSHINE, WARM

THE SUN ______ ON THE EARTH.
THE SUN ______ THE PLANTS GROW.
THE SUNSHINE IS ______.
THE SUN MAKES THE ______ GROW.
THE ______ IS WARM.
THE SUN MAKES THE PLANTS ______.

WRITE AND LEARN TO SPELL THESE WORDS:
SUN, SUNSHINE, SHINE, GROW, WARM, MAKES, PLANTS

____

____

____

____

5. Worksheet—for second grade reading level.

should have some simple matching exercises, a few words to trace or copy, and a picture or the space to draw a picture. The second group may have sentences to copy or sentences with blanks to fill in from a choice of two words. The third group may have a space to write a sentence or two about the topic, some matching words and pictures, or blanks to fill in from a choice of not more than three words. There should also be some words to spell and to use in sentences.

The junior high school and the high school pupils should have this same type of unit work, only on more specific topics selected for more mature interests and related in a large measure to the subjects their peers are studying. Lessons prepared for the older group will be on an interest level corresponding to their chronological age, but still commensurate with their mental age and ability level.

Materials for all age groups should be thoroughly screened or rewritten to make them simple and understandable. *The educable mentally retarded do not readily grasp any new idea.*

Procedure. The outline for the procedure should include an account of the manner in which the unit will be initiated and suggestions for initiating the studies of various areas.

The procedure should include the methods by which the unit will be developed through activities, experiences, and the integration of all of the areas involved in the study. The objectives for each area to be included in the entire unit should be stated under this part of the outline.

The procedure finally should include the culminating activities of the unit.

Evaluation. The teacher should carefully evaluate each lesson and, at the close of the unit, evaluate the entire study. This should be done while the responses and discussions are fresh in mind. She should note the strength, the weakness, the high and low point of interest, and the parts needed to be reviewed or enlarged upon.

This evaluation will influence the lesson plan for the following day. Some changes may be required, since each lesson plan must be based on the knowledge, skills, attitudes, and concepts that have been established.

6. Worksheet—for primary level.

The Bibliography. The bibliography should include complete information on the sources of everything used in connection with the unit. An annotated bibliography will be the most useful to the teacher for future reference.

INTEGRATION WITH OTHER AREAS

After the teacher has decided upon the general objectives for her study, she must survey all of the areas of learning and decide which ones would contribute helpful material for the attainment of these objectives. In building a unit she should avoid overlooking some potent possibility; yet she should not be a slave to form and attempt to include everything. There must be a specific reason or list of objectives directly connected with the study for each area that is included.

The Language Arts and the Social Science must be woven into a pattern of functional value to the children. Practical problems must be developed for arithmetic from the arts and crafts, homemaking and shop areas, as well as from the social science area.

Language Arts in the Modified Core Curriculum. The Language Arts are usually considered to include reading, oral and written language, spelling, and writing. These provide the medium in a core unit for the children to learn to use the basic skills as they are imbedded in a body of other useful knowledge.

Oral Language in the Core Curriculum Unit. Greater fluency in using oral language may be developed by means of experience stories or sharing periods. Sometimes it is wise to overlook grammatical errors if a child is doing well with his story. However, correct usage of the English language should be emphasized constantly in all work throughout the day.

Correct oral language may also be taught by simple dramatization that appears spontaneous. The use of a few props and the unit materials will achieve the effect desired. Such dramatizations could include practice in using the telephone, welcoming visitors to the room or to the home, entertaining visitors, making introductions, saying good-by to host or guests, or shopping at the school store. The teacher should instruct the children carefully so that there is no loss of self-confidence through corrections during these dramatizations.

Written Language in the Core Curriculum. Correct usage in writing is best learned by practice. Experience charts provide an opportunity for the teacher to show the use of capital letters, periods, commas, quotation marks, question marks, titles, and paragraphs.

The teacher makes use of every opportunity for the children to write letters of inquiry, invitation, and thanks. These activities provide excellent motivation for experience in using new vocabulary, as well as new skills.

The children should write or be helped to write stories of their own experiences. They must be taught how to make a sentence and a paragraph and when and where to punctuate and use capital letters. These stories furnish reading materials which may later be illustrated by drawings or paintings by the children.

The educable mentally retarded children should acquire enough experience and ability to enable them to take down information over the telephone, to make out a receipt, to prepare a shopping list, or to write a friendly letter.

Sometimes the teacher is able to locate published materials that will sustain interest until a basic vocabulary can be established; however, usually the teacher must prepare these materials. Although the interest level may be that of a ten or thirteen-year-old child, the content of the reading material could be as low as a readiness stage necessitating much oral language and practice on pre-primer material. This material is easily adapted from the unit being studied.

As long as the child is in the reading readiness stage, he should not be forced to recall words. However, as soon as he has sufficient muscle coordination to trace, he may begin tracing letter and word forms. He can *draw* the letter or word forms, and, as he does this, he begins to realize that these forms have different shapes.

Thus, it is possible the child may learn to write his name without knowing the letters in the name or being able to write other words. Learning to write his name is very important to the mentally retarded child.

Eventually the child will learn a basic sight vocabulary and the names of the letters of the alphabet. As he learns to read and as he matures, he should learn the alphabet in sequence. This will enable him to learn to locate words in lists and directories.

While the child is emerging from the readiness stage, he is able to make good progress in oral language. Through the unit study he is acquiring knowledge that enables him to enter into discussions with his classmates and with friends of his own chronological age. This gives him status with his peers.

READING IN THE CORE CURRICULUM

Mental Age and Readiness. The child of average intelligence is expected to begin reading at the chronological age of six or six and one-half years. To achieve success, he should be well physically and mentally.

The educable mentally retarded child at that chronological age may have a mental age of three to four years. He will not be ready to read until his mental age approaches the chronological age for usual children to begin to read. In the meantime he is in school, and if he is fortunate enough to have been recognized early, he will be in a special room. There he will be having an intensive readiness program. This program will include readiness for every area of living, as well as for the basic subjects of the language arts and arithmetic.

If the child is in a regular room and the teacher is aware of his difficulty, she may prepare special materials for him. The teacher in the regular room may not be aware of the child's retardation and think of him as being stubborn or lazy. She will attempt to have him make progress with the group. This will result in frustration and an intense dislike for school.

Educable mentally retarded children are usually eight to ten years of age chronologically before they are ready for formal reading. They may know a few words and have some experience with charts and primers before that age.

The educable mentally retarded child, as well as the normal child, has many problems that complicate his ability to understand and to retain concepts. The normal child, because of his ability to reason and arrive at sound judgments, is able to overcome his problems or to accept them philosophically and to be able to proceed with his education in a satisfactory manner. The mentally retarded child is overpowered by similar obstacles because he is unable to complete a solution to his problem.

The teacher must be understanding of this child's problem and his intense feeling of frustration. She must remember that the educable mentally retarded child cannot be hurried or coerced into learning, and that he will progress at his own rate of speed, depending upon his physical, social, emotional, and intellectual maturity.

Reading Motivation in the Core Curriculum. The mentally retarded child has usually had several frustrating years of being unsuccessfully exposed to reading. When the period of readiness arrives, the teacher must assume the responsibility for proper motivation.

The child will seldom respond to a re-hash of the primer or first reader he has been using for the past two or three years. Therefore, the teacher must find something that will hold his attention. This may be a thrilling story about the past or the present, or it may be a topic in which the child has indicated an interest. These subjects will fit into the unit plan and provide the proper motivation for the child's reading program.

A science demonstration or a story about animals frequently will hold the interest of the group and provide another subject that may be integrated into the core curriculum unit plan. The manner of introducing the subject is important. *The teacher's interest and enthusiasm cannot be overemphasized.* Without the spark that she alone can provide, the presentation will fail.

Once the child's interest in reading has been aroused, progress is much easier. However, to insure continued progress, the teacher should keep the content of the reading material simple, practical, and geared to the child's level of interest and comprehension.

Methods for the Reading Readiness Program in the Core Curriculum. The educable mentally retarded child who is not ready to read requires special training in visual and auditory imagery, in coordination and in rhythms, in social situations, and in storytelling. This child needs many new experiences that are carefully arranged from simple walks about the school building to trips to the neighborhood store, a fire station, a farm, or creamery. These activities may be integrated into the core unit to help the child achieve self-sufficiency.

Reading Readiness Activities for the Core Curriculum. The children should be encouraged to participate in the following activities to develop a readiness for reading:

1. Take an excursion around the school building.
2. Listen to a short story.
3. Look at a picture and tell a story.
4. Place pictures in order of sequence.
5. Dictate a story.
6. Learn where clock's hands point at noon.
7. Make story books from pictures cut out of magazines.
8. Take excursions to places out of the school building.
9. Make drawings of experiences.
10. Learn simple songs.
11. Play rhythms on simple instruments.
12. Learn simple rhymes.
13. Learn finger plays for jingles.
14. Play with big blocks.
15. Learn simple games.
16. Solve simple jigsaw puzzles.
17. Play house or store.
18. Learn simple health and safety habits.

Developing the Ability to Observe Visually. The teacher should show the pupils how to take part in the following activities to develop better visual awareness of their environment.

1. From a description of an object in the room have some child guess what it is.
2. Act out directions.
3. Match colors.
4. Match shapes.
5. Match sizes.
6. Match objects.
7. Name the objects in a box that were exposed briefly. Increase number of objects as the child becomes more proficient. Change the objects frequently.

8. Play games like ring toss or bean bags.
9. Take a walk and list the things seen.

Developing Auditory Perception. The teacher may assist the children to learn about sounds from these activities:

1. Listen to sounds to identify the source.
2. Listen to musical tones to identify high and low notes.
3. Listen to identify beginning sounds of words.
4. Find pictures of these words and make a scrapbook.
5. Listen for rhyming words.
6. Make up little jingles.

Developing Coordination and Rhythm. The children will be helped in developing coordination and a sense of rhythm through practicing the following activities:

1. Saying nursery rhymes with finger play activity.
2. Choral reading.
3. Echoing.
4. Rhythm band activities with records or piano.
5. Clapping, skipping, hopping to music.
6. Singing alone and in groups.
7. Playing games requiring throwing, running, jumping, and walking.
8. Cutting out pictures.
9. Coloring within lines.
10. Painting; finger painting.
11. Playing house.

There are many ways to help the child achieve reading readiness. These few ways are listed to illustrate the types of help the educable mentally retarded need to develop this readiness for reading.

SUMMARY

The teacher of the educable mentally retarded will find that the possibilities for using the framework of a modified core curriculum plan for units of work are varied, interesting, and challenging.

By modifying the unit plan to meet the group's requirements, she is able to introduce realistic situations and activities that are beneficial and stimulating to the children. All of them are able to take part in this kind of unit so that it becomes a real group activity.

Methods for integrating the Language Arts skills with other areas of learning are suggested.

The modified core curriculum units may be based upon social science integrated with the other areas of learning and with additional instruction in the basic skills. This presents an excellent plan whereby the educable mentally retarded may acquire adequate knowledge and skill to become self-sufficient, socially acceptable, appreciative of pleasant human relationships, and able to accept limited responsibility.

4

TEACHING TECHNIQUES AND GENERAL EXPERIENCES

THE UNIT AS A COMPLETE EXPERIENCE

A UNIT should provide a complete experience for the child educationally and emotionally. Some of the expected outcomes are learning basic skills, acquiring useful information, and achieving individual success and satisfaction.

As progress is achieved in a study, certain techniques for presentation will facilitate the retention of information.

The teacher will introduce materials and content to the group. This may be followed by a period of discussion. As the subject develops, the pupils will mention pertinent facts which should be listed on the chalk board. The result of such a list should be a story which the teacher writes as the pupils tell it. The story should be read by the pupils. Then it is copied for their booklets.

The next day new or useful words are presented on flash cards. The words may also be written on the chalk board and pronounced by the class.

The pupils may read the story from their copies. The teacher should check the papers to see if the copying is legible and accurate.

METHODS FOR TEACHING THE UNIT AND THE BASIC SKILLS

The story, which has been written on strips of paper, may then be cut into short phrases and individual words. As the words are shown to the class, the children choose the ones they recognize and build sentences in the wall chart. Many games may be played with the words to ensure retention. *It takes many, many exposures for the retention of a word.*

There must be visual, auditory, and kinesthetic knowledge of the word to make it useful in oral and written language. As the teacher of the educable mentally retarded listens to a child relate a story he has seen on television or heard on the radio, she gains immeasurable satisfaction in recalling that he liked the story because he had learned about one of the characters in school.

AUDIO-VISUAL AIDS IN THE UNIT

Audio-visual aids should be used wherever possible in presenting materials to mentally retarded children. The bulletin board is an important interest center. Proper displays have been discussed in another section, as have the audio-visual, writing and spelling methods and materials.

EXPERIENCE CHARTS

Experience charts are simply stories dictated by the children or prepared by the teacher. These charts, which are printed on lined chart paper, cards, or on the chalk board, are made day by day as the lessons progress. They are excellent for reviewing for content, increasing speed in reading, and assisting in vocabulary retention.

FLASH CARDS FOR WORD DRILL

Flash cards to match the experience charts must be made daily to aid in quick recognition of vocabulary. Health and safety words should also be displayed frequently to keep the child acquainted with words necessary for self-preservation, such as *danger, exit, stop, walk, go, enter, poison, one way, do not enter.* This task may be speeded by proper equipment consisting of lined chart paper, lined sentence strips for flash cards, and felt-tipped pens for lettering. These materials also aid in securing legible uniform lettering in a minimum of time.

ACTIVITIES FOR DRILL

In a word recognition game the children enjoy raising their hands when they know a word and coming to the teacher to claim it. They like to be allowed to build sentences and, later, to read them to the class.

The sentences on the long strips of paper may be cut apart into words and phrases and the children allowed to build them back a word at a time. There is keen rivalry for the word in the set of cards that has the period on it, for the possessor of that card may be allowed to read the reassembled sentence.

Another way to hold interest in remembering words is to place the words face down in a box. A child selects a card. If he knows the word, he gets to keep it. If he does not know it, he holds it up for someone else to recognize. Every child has a chance to have at least one word. The teacher should prepare picture cards for the children who are in the readiness group, thus assuring personal recognition, which is a big factor in reading success. Sentence strips may be presented to the group for reading. Prompt help should be provided if a child falters.

TO IMPROVE SIGHT VOCABULARY

A list of words on the chalk board should be used as a review or as a drill on new words. The class is divided into two groups. Each side chooses a word from the list. The teacher writes the words again on the board and appoints leaders. Each leader chooses someone from his side who plays a version of tic-tac-toe with his opponent. They try to see which side can cancel across first by using the chosen words which must be spelled and pronounced correctly each time. Different words and new leaders are chosen for the next game. These leaders may sometimes be the children who can not read or write.

The Word Wheel. Mentally retarded children enjoy a version of the word wheel in learning new words. Each child makes a wheel from heavy paper with a paper fastener in the center so that it will turn easily. Under a small window in the top section the words are written so they will show through the window. For the beginner the words may be written consecutively as in a familiar sentence or rhyme. When the child has learned the process and is sure of the words as he turns the wheel, he may play the game with the same words but in a different order. Later a new word may be mixed with familiar words.

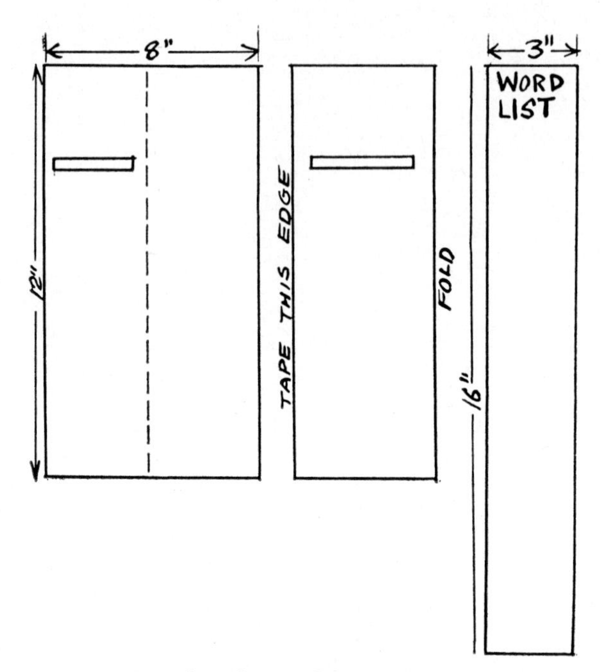

7. The Tachistoscope.

The Tachistoscope. The tachistoscope is also a helpful device to use in drill for word retention and quick recognition. This may be easily made from a strip of tag board folded lengthwise with a window cut in one side. The open lengthwise edges of the cardboard are taped together. The words are typed or written on strips of paper. These strips are drawn through the folded cardboard. The child pronounces the word as it appears in the window.

The strip of paper with the word list should be several inches longer than the tachistoscope or the holder for it. A card with a window the size of one line may also be made to fit over a page in a book or over a large chart. This is a help to poor readers, as it enables them to concentrate on a particular line or a part of a line.

Card Games. Card games similar to *Old Maid* are useful in improving visual discrimination and building sight vocabulary. The cards are made in pairs, except the odd card, which may

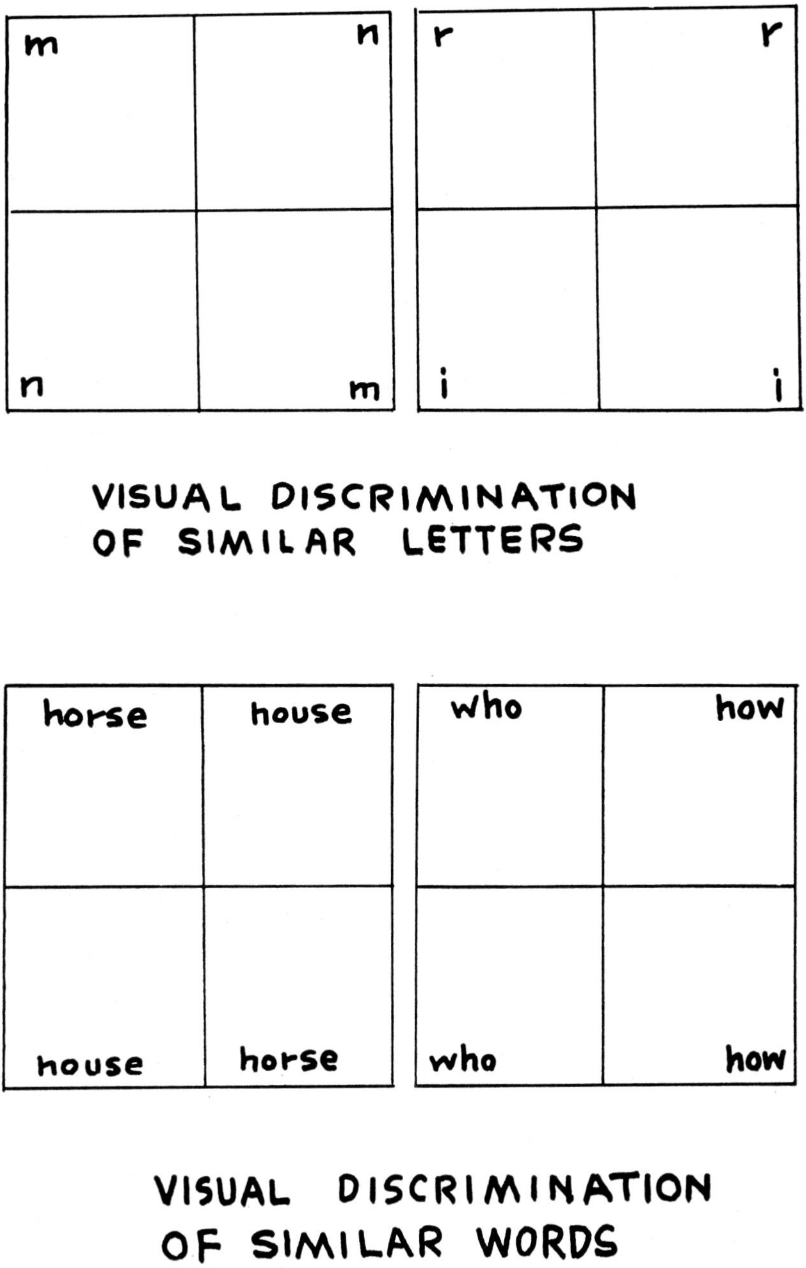

m n r r

n m i i

VISUAL DISCRIMINATION
OF SIMILAR LETTERS

horse house who how

house horse who how

VISUAL DISCRIMINATION
OF SIMILAR WORDS

8. Visual discrimination.

have a different word each time. The cards may be made from lightweight cardboard, such as tag board, or cardboard from the laundry. The words to be learned are typed on the cards. When the set of words has been learned, they may be blacked out and another set of words typed just below that line. The cards may be used many times in this way.

Many different ways may be found to vary the idea of word games, such as "Climbing the Ladder," "The Stepping Stones," or "Climbing the Stairs." These are all helpful aids in holding interest in a word drill.

VISUAL DISCRIMINATION

Sets of words or letters may be arranged in irregular sequence and dittoed for matching, finding similarities, and marking certain words or letters for visual discrimination.

Jigsaw puzzles are also good for this kind of training. The beginner may have a picture or a symbol cut in two parts. When he can match those, the same picture may be cut into three parts and later into four or five parts. Using large, clear, simple objects will eliminate unnecessary confusion.

Similar and Dissimilar Words and Letters. To assist in visual discrimination, the teacher may make sets of flash cards showing similar and dissimilar sets of letters or words. As a spare time project the children may be allowed to make their own sets of cards or other materials.

The teacher shows the children how to use a ruler, a pencil, squared paper, and a printing set. The one-inch squared paper is a good size to use for ruling off four squares into a 2 x 2 inch box. Using the teacher's cards as models, the children print the letters in the squares.

The teacher may also print difficult words in pairs on squares of paper for recognition. She should prepare similar material on the ditto for the children to use.

The teacher may cut words apart for the beginners in reading to reassemble. At first the child needs a pattern, which will be discarded as he improves.

VISUAL AND AUDITORY DISCRIMINATION

Lotto games may be made by the pupils. Pictures from magazines may be pasted onto paper in squares drawn on the paper. These may be used for the recognition of beginning sounds of words, vowels, endings, or other skills that suit the children's need. Disks or small squares of paper may also be used for markers. The one who secures a straight line of words across the page may read the sounds, words, or other correct answers. Words for drill may also be made into a lotto game.

CONFUSION WORDS AND LETTERS

Words and letters of the alphabet that are confusing to children may be used in drills for recognition and comprehension. The confusing words and letters may be printed on cards for proper identification. They may also be placed in squares, and, as the teacher pronounces one and uses it in a sentence, the children circle the correct word or letter.

SPEECH DEFECTS

Children with marked speech defects should have systematic speech training under a speech correctionist. The regular teacher may also help improve speech habits by insisting that words be pronounced correctly.

MARKERS FOR READING

Markers are useful in giving the child confidence in knowing where he is reading. If he does not have to worry about which line he is using, he is able to concentrate on looking at the words and interpreting them into visual concepts.

ORAL READING

The educable mentally retarded child should be allowed to read orally, because he needs this reinforcement of visual and auditory imagery for retention. Oral reading will help the child to gain confidence in his own ability. The teacher will assure him frequently that as long as she does not help him pronounce a word, he is reading correctly. Oral reading provides the teacher with a means of checking the child's reading for fluency, rhythm, and pronunciation.

COMPREHENSION

After the child has read a story, he should be urged to tell the story to someone in the class, or to the teacher. The teacher should ask questions about the story for comprehension. This also assists in retention of the facts of the story.

Exercises relating to stories or class work should be prepared by the teacher. These may consist of short sentences with blanks for inserting words from a list; words to use in sentences with the missing word indicated by dots corresponding to the number of letters in the correct word; simple questions to be answered with a sentence including a word from a given list; questions to be answered with a complete sentence with no list of words given; and directions to be followed. This material should be prepared at several levels of difficulty from beginning reading to the highest level in the class.

EXERCISES FOR COMPREHENSION

Examples of exercises for comprehension and retention are given here as suggestions for work that the teacher should use in developing the unit for integration in all areas.

Directions to Follow

1. Draw a cloud.
2. Draw the sun. Color the sun yellow.
3. Draw a tree. Color the tree green.
4. Draw a tree in the wind.
5. Draw a tree in summer.
6. Draw a tree in winter.

Sentences for Comprehension

1. Where is a safe place when lighting is near?
2. What two kinds of lightning do you usually see?
3. Is the North Star always in the North?
4. In what direction do you look to see the sun of a morning?
5. What are some of the uses for water?

Individual Reading Assignment

Read this story and fill in the blanks.

SPRING

The class went for a walk to the school farm.
We saw a tractor and a plow.
We saw baby chickens, a cow, and a calf.
We knew that spring had come.
We saw a tractor and a ....
We saw ...., a cow and ....
We knew that .... had come.
Learn to spell baby, chickens, calf, spring, plow.

Flash Cards. The teacher should prepare flash cards illustrating opposites and words that are difficult to understand. These cards, which are used in the presentaion of all new words in the stories and for review of other vocabulary, should have large print.

Labels as an Aid to Word Recognition. Labels on objects used in presenting the unit are an aid to word recognition. The lettering should be simple manuscript writing that corresponds to the regular letter forms which are taught the children. Doors, windows, chairs and other objects about the room may have signs on them. The teacher should be cautious about putting up too many labels at one time, for they may lose their effectiveness.

GENERAL EXPERIENCES

Preparation for the First Day of School. The teacher of a group of educable mentally retarded children must plan wisely for each child and for each minute of the day. Before school starts in the fall, she should set up a timetable for such items as report cards, parent conferences, P.T.A. meetings, faculty meetings, room meetings with parents, and professional meetings. This will enable her to prepare adequately for her work ahead of such events.

Supplies for the room should be unpacked and stored ready for use. These should include crayons, pencils, paints, drawing paper, news print, puzzles, games, picture books, building blocks, dominoes, checkers, Lincoln logs, scissors and paste. The teacher will be able with such materials to keep a group of young or intermediate age pupils occupied while she becomes acquainted with them.

Pupils' Check List

Pupils' Names	M	T	W	TH	F	M	T	W	TH	F
Larry										
Gary										
Brenda										
Troy										
Sue										
James										
Jeanette										
Steven										
Janice										
Rene										

9. Pupils' check list.

The older mentally retarded group are young people who are mature enough to be directed into many activities. Their schedule is usually varied enough to keep them busy the first day.

Pupils' Check List. The daily schedule should be prepared ahead of the first day of school and be posted on the chalk board or bulletin board. The pupils names may be prepared on a sheet for dittoing. Names listed with spaces following for daily records, make a simple and convenient form for many check lists and reports.

When the children are known to the teacher before school starts, she may prepare fresh name plates and fasten them to the front of the desks with masking tape. She may also prepare a chart listing duties for the children and a seating chart before the first day of school.

The First Day of School. The teacher should have the room in order and well outlined plans for many activities for the first day of school. That is the most demanding day of the school year.

Much of the success of the following weeks depends upon the impression the children receive of the teacher on the first day of school.

If the children's names are on their desks, it is easy to recognize and use their names. This a good device to help the children get acquainted. They appreciate this recognition.

In order to know each other better the children might relate their vacation experiences. The teacher in turn should be prepared to review her holiday. If she has brought some souvenirs or pictures to share with them, the children will receive greater enjoyment from her report.

A child who is new to the room may be seated near a more mature pupil, who will act as a counselor. The new pupil may ask the counselor for help in pronouncing words or the names of letters in a word. The boys and girls soon understand that this arrangement is not for visiting or playing. Children are often very good teachers, for they remember their own difficulties and are able to put into words an explanation that conveys the idea perfectly to the other child.

The teacher should take time to explain her few basic rules for the group's conduct, the daily schedule of classes and activities, and the room monitors' or helpers' duties.

The teacher should keep the children occupied by attempting to hear some of them read, doing some arithmetic and starting plans for a social study unit. Since the children will be eager to get back into the routine of the school work, they should not be disappointed, but be allowed to do some work at their level of ability.

On the first day of school a tour of the building and the grounds is in order. After new pupils learn what takes place in other parts of the building, they will have less incentive to go wandering about alone.

The children should be shown where to take reports, where to mail letters, where to get the teacher's mail, and where the principal's office is located. They should also get acquainted with the caretaker if he is on duty.

Fire Drill Routine. The route for evacuating the school building in an emergency is usually known in advance of the beginning of school. The teacher should use part of the first day of school to help the children become familiar with the fire drill routine. She should impress upon the children the fact that, since they were just practicing, there is no real danger present.

The various steps in leaving the room and getting safely to the playground should be rehearsed orally several times before the actual attempt to follow through with a drill by the group. There should be at least three complete fire drills the first day. This means the route should be covered exactly each time as it should be done if there was an emergency. The routine, once established, should not be changed in future drills unless an alternate emergency route must be taught as a safety precaution. The children should be taken over the new evacuation route *only* after the first one has been mastered.

The teacher should assign an older responsible child to walk with a younger, fearful, or physically handicapped child in order to reassure and to assist him.

Sometimes the children may be out of the classroom in some other area when a fire drill signal sounds. It should be impressed upon them that they are to go from the building with the person in charge of them at that time. The teacher must make the children understand that *they are not to come back to the home room* for any reason. The teacher should make this a stern command, "Never, never, come back to the room for anything during a fire drill."

A mentally retarded child often becomes attached to some object—a book, a box of crayons, a shell—and may try to return to the room to retrieve it.

The teacher of the educable mentally retarded should be the one who is responsible for closing the windows and the doors. She should search the rest room so that no child may be left in the building. She should then follow the group out of the room and count the children as soon as possible after they are out of the building. If one child is missing, she should leave the group with a responsible person and return to find the child.

Since a fire drill is an emotional experience for children, they should be closely guided and guarded from the time the fire alarm sounds until they are safely back in the room. The educable mentally retarded children must be so well trained that habit takes over in an emergency; otherwise, they will panic and be a menace to other children as well as to themselves.

Delegating Routine Tasks. The teacher should assign the room duties and assure everyone that these will be rotated so that some time during the year each one will be a helper for each duty.

10. Delegating room tasks.

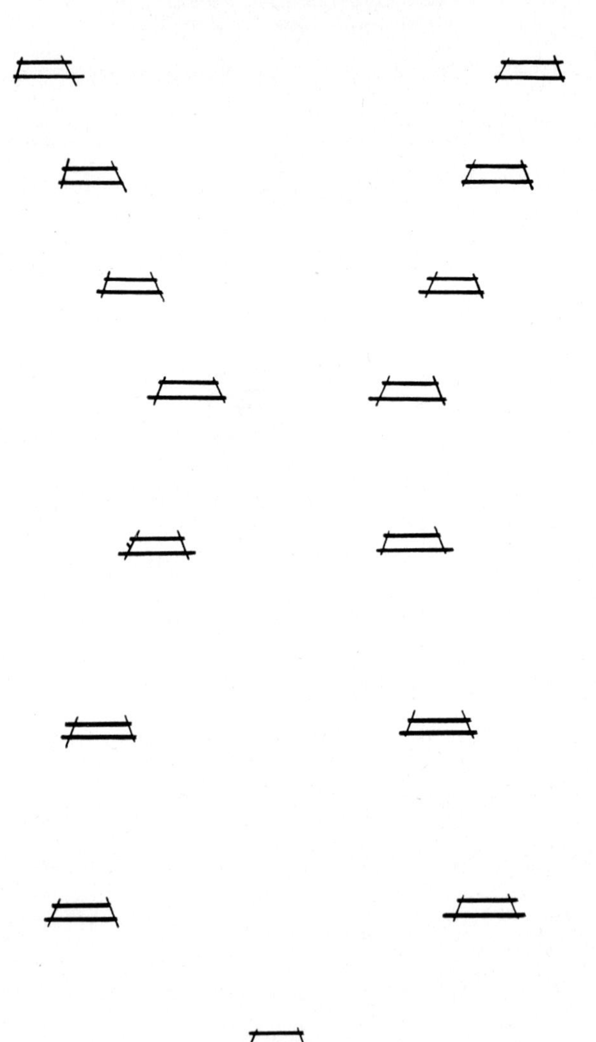

11. Attendance records—open seating.

Attendance Records
STAGGERED SEATING

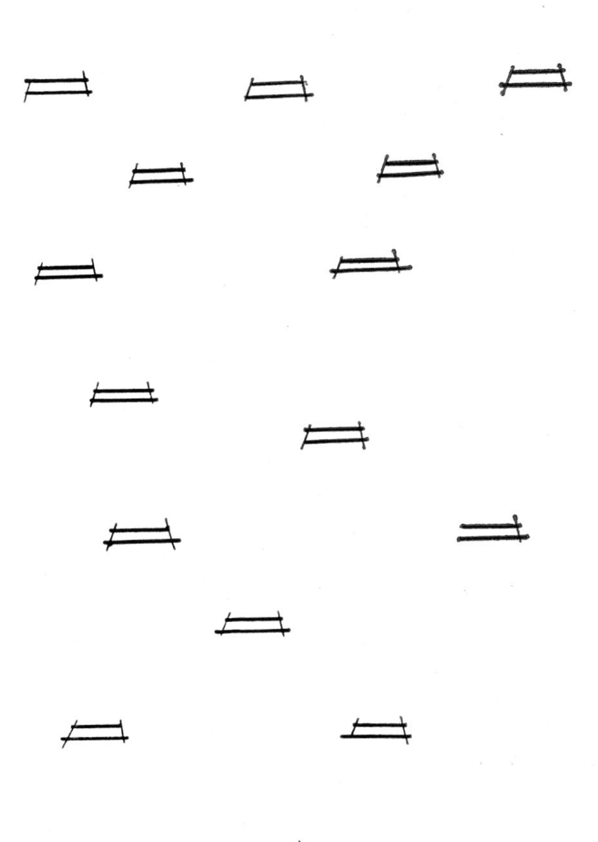

12. Attendance records—staggered seating.

Each child's name may be printed on a strip of paper with a felt-tipped pen. The strips of paper with the names on them may be attached to the chart listing the room duties. Special adhesive plastic disks, which may be used on the paper, allow the teacher to reassign duties without rewriting the pupils' names.

The room duties may be as numerous as the children in the room or limited to make the helper an envied person. The list might include taking attendance reports to the office, passing the wastebasket, serving lunch, and collecting the lunch money.

The children, who quickly learn where supplies are kept, are adept at passing out materials as they are needed. Since the children take pride in doing these things, they should be allowed to do as many as they can learn to do well.

Training a child to perform a routine correctly is time-consuming, but it is worth the time and effort in saving the teacher steps, and in giving the child the personal satisfaction derived from this small responsibility.

The appointment of one of the older children as a room librarian offers an opportunity for the use of good writing ability. A child who is willing and able to be gracious, yet persistent, in collecting the books will be a good librarian.

Carrying out room duties helps to develop such qualities as a feeling of confidence in one's ability, satisfaction in carrying out an assignment, dependability, punctuality, and cooperativeness.

Responsibility for Attendance Reports. The teacher should prepare a simple seating chart by using a small pocket chart in which she places the children's name cards in positions corresponding to their seats in the room. The desks have been previously labeled with the children's names.

A pupil helper may take the attendance record and report it to the office. He will soon learn how to check the chart and the desks. He can copy the absentee's name from the desk, remove the corresponding card from the chart and place it on the teacher's desk for her convenience in recording the absentee's name in her record book.

Simple Room Routine. Before school starts each morning, the teacher should have a lesson plan prepared with materials and equipment ready for carrying out the scheduled activities. The materials should be located conveniently to eliminate the necessity of leaving the class unsupervised. Interesting and constructive individual work should be available when the group activity has been completed.

The teacher should be careful to present any work in the same way she expects it to be completed. The routine of the daily activities should be kept simple. Confusion can be avoided by anticipating necessary changes.

As soon as the children gain confidence in the teacher and acquire a feeling of belonging to the group, the teacher may talk to them about room privileges. They should be told that certain things may be done without asking for permission, such as sharpening a pencil, going to the rest room, or getting a drink.

Impress upon the children that one rule must be observed: *Only one child may be walking about at a time.* This helps the children acquire a sense of group responsibility. It also prevents many time-consuming interruptions for the teacher and other members of the class.

Temperature and Ventilation of the Room. The physical aspect of the classroom is important in management and discipline. If the children become restless and start moving about, or a buzz develops, the teacher must interrupt her routine at once and seek the cause. The air in the room may be too hot or too cold, the light for desk work may be too glaring or too dim, or the children may need a change of activity.

Relaxation for the Pupils. The teacher should attempt to reduce tension or restlessness in the pupils by introducing different conditions and experiences. She may adjust the lights or ventilation and proceed to initiate some group activity. This may be a game such as "Do What I Do," in which any activities performed by the leader are imitated by the entire group.

Choral readings and finger plays with rhymes are relaxing. The teacher can read the rhyme, and the children will soon learn it as they act it out. They enjoy chanting a refrain or being an echo. After five or ten minutes of relaxation the pupils should be ready to return to their regular assignments.

13. The Grocery Store.

Seat Activities. When the children are through with the skill subjects, they often have some time with nothing special to occupy their minds or hands. The teacher should have material available for some purposeful activity.

For the younger group these may include perception materials for training discrimination in likenesses and differences, tracing materials for training letter and number form recognition, and simple games and puzzles.

The intermediate group may have number and word games, clay for modeling, paints and paper for painting, and simple craft activities.

The older groups of mentally retarded should not have a surplus of time, since they are busy with vocational training, as well as with regular academic and non-academic activities.

There should be one definite restriction concerning the use of the above mentioned materials. The children must complete their assigned lessons to the best of their ability before they are free to use the extra materials. The teacher may make quick spot checks to assure herself that the children are not abusing the privilege of this free, quiet activity.

Experiences. First-hand experiences are best remembered by any child. This is especially true of the mentally retarded. There should be practice in the school room with many lifelike situations. The lunch period provides an opportunity for a real experience. Another first-hand situation is the field trip, where processes or objects may be viewed in their natural setting.

Devices may be used in the classroom to imitate first-hand experiences. One such helpful device is the store within the classroom. The children may set up the store with counters, shelves, shopping carts, or bags. They may change the kind of merchandise displayed to provide new experiences. The store may become a grocery store, a pet shop, a hat shop, or a filling station. The shelves and counters may be rearranged to accommodate the new labels and containers or pictures of articles for sale.

By learning how to buy and sell different articles, the children will see a practical use of money and learn the value of knowing how to make correct change. They learn how to interpret weights and measures, how to use the telephone correctly, how to tell time, and how to compare prices and values.

In connection with such studies, auditory and visual aids should be used as frequently as possible. These should include films, filmstrips, recordings, field trips, pictures, and models. The children may also work with many materials and achieve a finished product.

The teacher must be responsible for arousing the interest and understanding for activities she initiates. The educable mentally retarded have little knowledge of materials or topics available for study. Since the children's experiences are usually limited on these matters, the teacher is only hampering the program by prolonged planning with the group; however, she must follow through on ideas suggested by the children wherever it is feasible. By keeping assignments within the level of their ability, she can win their confidence so that she is in a position to offer help where it is needed.

Activities Scaled to Ability. When the teacher starts to work with a new pupil, she has difficulty in determining his ability level in the various areas. She is eager to start him at as high a level as possible. The child usually agrees with any suggestion made by the teacher about where to start reading, whether in first or third grade material. Therefore, he should be tested for correct placement before being given an assignment.

The teacher of the educable mentally retarded in any situation must be alert to the child's need for assistance in academic, as well as in art and craft work. If the academic material or any other activity seems to be causing frustration, she should assist the child to complete the lesson or article.

If this cannot be managed, the child's sense of failure may cause a serious emotional block to his future development. In any case, to help prevent such an occurrence, she should start another activity for him scaled to a lower level. He should be urged and helped to complete this activity so that he feels successful. The teacher's smile of approval for his little achievement will make him want to try again.

14. Boys working at crafts in the classroom.

Giving Directions. When working with the educable mentally retarded, the teacher should outline and explain the activity step by step until he is able to carry out the work unaided. He will then achieve confidence and satisfaction in performing alone.

To avoid confusion in the children's minds, the teacher should state one thing only and explain that. She should question the children to determine their understanding of the statement or directive. It is never safe to assume that the mentally retarded know or understand anything. Because they have been conditioned to rejection for being ignorant, they remain mute. Frequently a commonly used word, such as *over,* needs an explanation which must be taught and retaught until the meaning has become a part of the child's vocabulary. Along with the problem of learning to use simple terms, they have great difficulty in understanding directions.

For their future success as employees, the educable mentally retarded must be taught to follow directions implicitly. Since these children need so much assistance in learning any activity or procedure, the teacher must have patience as well as persistence. She must also know the value of securing complete attention before starting to give any instruction.

Procedure for a Group Activity. As the teacher stands in front of the group, she should speak quietly, but firmly, and assume an attitude of expecting attention. She should request that the desks be cleared of all materials. After that has been done and the children are facing her, she is ready to begin her lesson.

The teacher should remember that the mentally retarded's attention span is short. She should be prepared to take instant advantage of that quiet hush when all of the children are looking at her to present something that will provide motivation for them to continue listening. It is also at such times that she may give most effectively the directions which are most likely to be remembered.

This procedure preparatory to any group activity should become automatic with teacher and pupils. These mentally retarded children are creatures of habit, who will always work under direct supervision. The teacher has the responsibility to instill the habit of following directions carefully and of completing assignments. The mentally retarded must acquire good working habits in order to become self-sufficient adults.

Procedure for a Choice of Activities. In speaking to the mentally retarded, the teacher should learn to be careful of her selection of words. A directive should be so plainly stated that the child has no doubt as to whether he has a choice or is expected to actually perform the request, which should be reasonable and consistent with the known performance ability of the child. The teacher should keep in mind the fact that the mentally retarded child is a literal-minded person. For example, if the teacher asks, "Would you like to play 'Green Light, Red Light'?" and the children say "No," she must suggest another game. If the teacher says, "Let us get ready to play 'Green Light, Red Light,'" there will be no confusion and most of the group will enjoy the game.

The teacher must be prepared to abide by the group's decision if she asks for a choice or an opinion. There are many times when the children should be allowed to make a choice. Training is required to help them to know the correct choices to make under various circumstances.

Promotion of Social Competence. To promote better understanding of human inter-relationships and social competence the teacher may direct the children in the following activities:

1. Building a play store, a miniature town, a play house.
2. Cultivating hobbies, such as taking pictures, making models, or collecting stamps.
3. Dramatizing the effects of diseases or unacceptable social behavior on a community by using puppets, peep shows, tableaux, shadow plays, pantomimes, and social dramas.
4. Learning about homemaking through cooking, canning, caring for equipment, dusting, cleaning, and doing the laundry.

15. The Post Office.

5. Having contacts with the doctor, dentist, nurse, and social worker.
6. Having daily inspection of hands, ears, nails, teeth, and skin.
7. Keeping records, of weight, height, and attendance.
8. Listening to the radio, TV, and records.
9. Learning the value of health and personality development by visiting the health center, the Red Cross, a hospital, and a guidance counselor.
10. Keeping a library corner in the classroom.
11. Learning the uses of pictures, maps, graphs, charts, specimens, and models.
12. Writing letters of friendship, invitation, and thank-you notes.
13. Modeling, painting, and drawing.
14. Making posters for health and safety studies.
15. Practicing shop activities, such as learning how to nail boards together, sawing a board along a straight line, measuring materials, and making simple repairs about the home.
16. Studying to discover how workers affect each other in their various areas: Firemen, policemen, transportation workers, farmers, clothing manufacturers, communication personnel, doctors, nurses, teachers and other community workers.
17. Taking excursions to talk with the people being studied about.
18. Using texts, books, magazines, and newspapers for information and pleasure.
19. Telling stories showing how to make friends and keep them.
20. Viewing films about health, safety, and community workers.
21. Weaving, sewing, and making other handcrafts.

Promotion of Economic Efficiency. The teacher should encourage the pupils to participate in those activities that will contribute to their feelings of success and security. Some suggestions follow for developing economic efficiency.

1. Maintaining good mental and physical health through games, modeling, a study of nutrition, and personal hygiene.
2. Learning muscular coordination through rhythms, dancing, games, and practice in walking, sitting, and standing correctly.

3. Learning the basic facts and skills in arithmetic.
4. Talking with people about jobs.
5. Using books, magazines, newspapers, records, and films.
6. Spelling useful words.
7. Dramatizing situations related to economic efficiency.
8. Matching objects.
9. Carrying on conversations personally and over the telephone.
10. Buying supplies.
11. Keeping records.
12. Telling stories to the class.
13. Reading stories silently and orally.
14. Reading signs.
15. Learning to follow directions.
16. Learning about banking procedures, such as cashing checks, paying notes, interest, and taxes.
17. Using charts, diagrams, and patterns.
18. Learning about applying for a job.

Promotion of Self-realization. The children may be guided in carrying out the following activities:

1. Acting as hosts or hostesses.
2. Developing hobbies.
3. Dramatizing events that will help develop self-realization by giving puppet shows, social dramas, peep shows, and historical plays.
4. Learning about buying food, clothing, furnishings, cars, and equipment.
5. Developing language through using the telephone, making introductions, and practicing conversation.
6. Learning new crafts, such as weaving, sewing, ceramics, or knitting.
7. Learning to enjoy music by listening, playing an instrument, leading or participating in rhythmic games or singing.
8. Observing and participating in community activities.
9. Performing experiments under careful supervision.
10. Participating in class discussions about reports, exhibits, plans, trips, class activities.

11. Participating in physical education programs of rhythms, games, exercises, and dances.
12. Reading for pleasure or information from want ads, sales, signs, and catalogs.
13. Sharing stories, experiences, and current events.
14. Using art materials for painting, modeling, and illustrating stories.
15. Writing letters, stories, notes, or filling out application forms.

Promotion of Civic-responsibility. The teacher should direct the pupils in the following activities to help develop a sense of civic-responsibility:

1. Study about the city, county, state, national, and world affairs through viewing pictures, films, television; reading books, magazines, newspapers, graphs, and charts.
2. Doing errands.
3. Writing to get information, to give information, and to carry on a correspondence.
4. Reading for information, protection, and pleasure.
5. Learning about the cost of our government.
6. Discussing responsibility for paying debts and current bills, taxes, and loans of a personal nature.
7. Locating through field trips and studying the uses of libraries, churches, YWCA, YMCA, parks, museums, recreation centers, fire stations, police station, city hall, county buildings, social security office, schools, banks, internal revenue office, utilities offices, factories, stores, hospitals, and special service organizations.

Value of Praise. The educable mentally retarded child should be encouraged to evaluate his work fairly. He has failed so often that he frequently remarks in advance of presenting his work, "It's not right. It's no good." He says this to preserve his ego if the teacher should find a mistake in his work. If this child has experienced the defeat of being in a regular room, he feels from previous experience that his paper will soon be covered with red marks denoting failure.

The teacher, before pointing out any mistakes on a paper, must find some opportunity to give the child a word of praise and encouragement. He must be reassured that he is loved and appreciated. The two may talk about something not related to school. Such a conversation could be more beneficial that day than an arithmetic lesson.

When the teacher does check the arithmetic paper and finds many examples are incorrect, she should not point out all of the errors at one time. Such mass failure overwhelms the child. If possible, she should find the correct ones and point them out to the child before showing an incorrect answer and explaining why it is wrong.

The teacher assumes the attitude that the child wants to do his work correctly and that he expects her to be the one to help him. She should be matter-of-fact about explaining the process so he understands it. If it is apparent the child is attempting to work with material too advanced for his ability, she should substitute other work sheets for him to do. The child should not be asked to erase incorrect answers to examples and re-work them. He should be given a clean work sheet and allowed to start again.

The teacher's attitude of fairness, interest, and firmness will usually overcome the child's tendency to defeatism in the face of criticism. The child's realization that everyone must learn to accept criticism when work has not been done correctly should lead him to want to remedy his errors and do work that will gain praise.

Stimulating Experiences for the Mentally Retarded. An educable mentally retarded child needs stimulation and assistance in understanding everything, far beyond the requirements of the usual child. He needs to learn that he must keep at the task to make progress. The teacher should know that he cannot be hurried or nagged; instead, he should be guided and stimulated. He should be helped to finish anything he starts so that he will have the satisfaction of completing a project. If he becomes tired and the teacher is not securing the response and interest she had planned, perhaps the lack of cooperation is in the teacher's enthusiasm, in the quality of the materials, or in the method of presentation.

To spare the child the feeling of defeat, the teacher should bring the unsatisfactory project to a close as quickly as possible

16. Social Studies.

and start on something that does have interest for both her and the pupil. The pupil's interest and enthusiasm will correspond to that generated by the teacher.

The educable mentally retarded, who thrive under kindly, stimulating supervision and teaching, are usually amenable to suggestions. The teacher must organize activities within their ability so that every child has an opportunity to be important. This applies to every area of contact, whether it is art and craft work, physical education, homemaking, shop work, supervised play period, library period, a unit of work, or basic skills. The ego of these children must be bolstered with activities that give them feelings of security and self-respect.

Importance of the Teacher. The teacher who is determined to hold with tradition in presenting any activity or experience to these children is doing them a grave disservice. Unless a teacher is willing to accept these mentally retarded as ones worthy of her

17. A Reading Lesson.

time in preparing suitable work and activities, she should get another position at once.

Though the potential of no person may be predicted accurately, due to the many physical, emotional and environmental factors that may be involved, these children, who are functioning within the range of the educable mentally retarded, must be regarded as, and taught as, mentally sub-normal children. If they are handled correctly, the pseudo-retarded may break through their barriers and begin to function closer to their true ability.

The importance of the teacher cannot be over-emphasized. She must be kind, loving, and sympathetic without being sentimental. She must be possessed of unlimited patience and perseverance. She must possess creativeness and enthusiasm, as well as a broad academic background. She may be young or old. These retarded children respect and love a teacher because of her attitude toward them, and because of the security and interesting experiences she gives to them.

Experiences Unfavorable for the Brain-Injured Mentally Retarded. The brain-injured child who is educable, but mentally retarded is frequently placed in a room for the educable mentally retarded. This is not conducive to his academic or emotional improvement, for his requirements are the opposite of the group in which he has been placed. The stimulation that is so necessary for success with the retarded is confusing, mentally and emotionally, to the brain-injured child. He requires a quiet room with special materials and techniques devised individually to meet his needs.

The classroom teacher who has this brain-injured child should be understanding when he becomes excited and talkative during regular class activities. She may provide him with the seclusion he requires by having a screen placed around his desk, or by excusing him from certain projects and allowing him to rest in another room.

DISCIPLINE FOR THE MENTALLY RETARDED

Discipline for a New Group. When a teacher is starting with a new class, her future success often depends upon beginning as a strict disciplinarian. After the children learn how to fit into the class routine, how to behave toward each other and the teacher, and how to cooperate and to work as a group, discipline may be relaxed. When the children forget or become careless about rules and liberties, discipline must again be enforced.

Trouble Symptoms. The trained teacher recognizes symptoms of trouble and is always alert to prevent its development. If there are confirmed trouble makers in the class, the teacher should not turn her back to the group. She must know what is going on at all times. She may avoid trouble by directing a special activity which removes the instigator from his immediate environment. The child may return a book to the library, adjust the ventilation, perform some duty in the work room, or work for a while with the paints or clay.

A session with paints or clay has a tendency to relieve pent-up inner feelings, provide for relaxation, and assist the child in regaining control of his emotions. Such activity must be entirely unsupervised to be of any value. The teacher should not seem curious about what the child is doing; however, if the child wishes to share what he has completed by showing it or talking about it, she should take the time to look and listen.

Control of a Group. The teacher can control the group more successfully with gestures and smiles than with spoken commands. She should talk only when the children should listen and speak clearly and only loudly enough to be heard throughout the room. Her directions should be in simple, but detailed form. When children know what the teacher expects them to do, they are usually happy to comply. The child who does not understand and is afraid of failure may be the cause of dissatisfaction among the others in the group.

Difficulties Between Pupils. When difficulties arise between pupils, it is seldom wise to force an issue before the class. The ones who have been having trouble should remain isolated until they have time to lose some of their anger and the teacher has had time to consider the matter objectively.

Since a child needs to save his dignity, the teacher should talk privately with each participant to get his own version of the story. Punishment, to be effective, should be suitable and immediate. After the punishment is completed, the child should resume his place in the class and be reassured by the teacher's attitude and actions that he has her love and trust.

Right and Wrong Behavior. Threats, arguments, and lectures are idle gestures with the mentally retarded. It is necessary to definitely teach that certain acts are good and right and that others are bad and wrong. They should learn that certain acts are socially acceptable, while others are not acceptable. *These children must be led and directed,* for *they are the followers in our world.*

TEACHER PARENT RELATIONSHIPS

Counseling with Parents. The teacher should be thoroughly familiar with the case history of each child in her group. She should know his social and economic background and his medical history, as well as his academic and psychological test results. Complete copies of all of this material should be in the files of the teacher, for her usefulness to the child depends upon her knowledge of his experiences. This confidential material should be provided for the teacher without her request and should be kept in a locked file.

After the teacher becomes acquainted with the child and his case history, she is in a position to talk with the parents in an intelligent manner. She is unable to offer constructive help if part of the child's life is kept secret from her. She needs to know whether the child is an epileptic, whether he is receiving medication, whether he is asthmatic, or whether he must have a special diet.

When the parents come to the school for their first conference with the teacher, she may establish good rapport if she can talk about the child's physical condition and then guide the discussion to the child's mental problems.

The teacher finds frequently that the parents have not been told or have not been convinced that the child is mentally retarded. They are worried and disturbed over his condition. The teacher is often the one who has the responsibility for counseling with the distracted parents and helping them adjust to the idea that the child will never be able to become the doctor or lawyer of their dreams. The teacher must guide them to accept the child and to love him for himself alone, rather than to reject him because of his disabilities.

Counseling with the parents may also help to win acceptance for the mentally retarded child in the family circle. Siblings frequently cause as much difficulty as parents in the emotional life of the mentally retarded child. The teacher should be able to direct the family to a mental health clinic where trained guidance can be given to prevent the disruption of a family.

Conferences with the parents should be arranged once each semester. If the school approves or requests home visits, these should be made in the early fall. Later the parents should come to the school for conferences. At that time the matters of health, regular atendance, discipline, plan of reporting progress, and room procedures and regulations should be explained by the teacher.

Much of the need for discipline will be eliminated if the teacher has established a cordial and sound relationship with the parents. After the teacher understands the parents' feelings, she can help them to understand their child. Most parents want to follow the plan that is best for the child.

Reporting Child's Progress. Reports on progress for the educable mentally retarded usually do not follow the same form as those used by the regular grades. There is no group competition for grades among the mentally retarded, for every child proceeds at his own rate of progress.

To satisfy the child and his parents, the teacher may send out a statement at regular intervals to coincide with the other reports from the school system. This is usually a summary of work done as a group, an evaluation of progress according to ability in the basic skills, a health report, and an attendance report.

Near the close of school the teacher may hold a second conference with the parents. If they are seen at meetings or other times, or if problems have been discussed over the telephone, the spring conference may be cancelled. At the close of school she sends a letter to the parents, which gives them detailed information concerning the child's progress and makes recommendations for the following term of school.

A Report to Parents

School ....

Report for ....

Date ....

Attendance: Days present .... Days absent ....

Reading, Writing, Spelling and Arithmetic are taught to your child on an individual basis or to small groups of children having comparable ability.

Reading	Social Studies	Library
Writing	Science	Industrial Arts for Boys
Spelling	Music	Homemaking for Girls
Arithmetic	Art	Social Progress
	Physical Education	

Lunch is served in the home room at noon with the supervising teacher in charge. The lunch period is followed by a supervised play period.

If you wish to discuss any problem, please call the supervising teacher who will arrange for a special conference. Your next regular conference date is listed below. Please write or call to confirm the date.

Date .... Day .... Hour ....

....

Supervising Teacher

SUMMARY

Ultimate Vocational Placement. The educable mentally retarded have a special place in the economy of our country. There are many essential jobs in every community and in industry for which they are especially well-fitted by temperament and ability.

These children must be given experiences to prepare them for real life situations. All of their daily activities and experiences comprise their curriculum. They must learn to follow directions, to work under supervision, to be punctual, to be honest, to assume responsibility for completing a task, to get along with others, to control their words and their actions, and to attend to their own affairs.

Where the teacher accepts the responsibility of instilling respect for authority and developing good mental health along with the teaching of the basic skills and social graces, the pupils will likely be employable. Industrial leaders have stated that the employment possibility of the mentally deficient is based largely upon their emotional stability and their ability to take orders from supervisors and to carry out directions.

Not all children classified as being educable mentally retarded will be able to utilize all of the training that is offered. However, to the extent that each person is able to do so, his life and the lives of his family are benefitted. Therefore, teachers should have patience, persistence, enthusiasm, and creativity. They must have academic ability and proficiency in many areas of teaching to work efficiently with these children who are handicapped with a poorly functioning brain. Teachers of the educable mentally retarded must be able to counsel and work with the parents, as well as the children, in order that these children will achieve ultimate permanent vocational placement.

5

UNITS OF WORK

MODIFIED CORE CURRICULUM UNITS

EXAMPLES of units using the modified core curriculum plan are given in this chapter to show how the basic skills are incorporated with the other areas of learning. These plans also present an adaptation of the outline for preparing units.

The first unit, "Summer Fun," illustrates the integration of the areas of learning and skills common to most elementary schools. The unit outline is adapted to meet the needs of the educable mentally retarded of intermediate age. The teacher should plan to take from two or four months' time to complete this unit.

The second unit, "The Weather," has a definite plan for fifteen days. It is developed from a list of questions the children asked during the study of "Summer Fun." This simple unit could be used by teachers who do not care for long units or for the core plan. Detailed lesson plans are included with the unit about the weather.

The third small unit was developed for the children whose interests in clouds went further than the unit about weather. The five lesson plans in this area show how to present a topic in a brief time. The elements for motivation are included in all of these plans in the presentation of the materials.

SUMMER FUN

I. Purpose.

To enrich the lives of the educable mentally retarded children, whose chronological ages are from ten through thirteen years, and whose mental ages are from five through eight years.

18. Bulletin board, flash cards, sentences, experience charts, drawing, booklets for the unit "Summer Fun."

II. Objectives.

A. To foster an appreciation of simple, orderly, pleasure in summer.

B. To learn how everyday living can be enjoyable.

C. To learn some healthful exercises for social skills and for recreation.

D. To learn to sing and to participate in games and dancing.

E. To learn to make useful articles that may be used in group situations such as picnics.

G. To learn to eat wisely in the summer and to prepare the right kind of food and drinks for lunches, picnics, and snacks.

H. To learn good grooming and correct costuming for summer outings and for home wear.

I. To learn how to make a simple costume for summer, a beach bag, beach pillow, place mats, coasters for drinks, hot dish mats, and some pottery for candy dishes or snacks.

J. To learn health and safety rules for outdoor play in summer.

K. To learn simple first aid.

L. To learn the skills of the basic subjects needed to carry out these objectives.

M. To achieve knowledge and skills as they relate to everyday living.

N. To assist in achieving self-realization, economic competency, good human relationships, and civic responsibility.

III. Integration with other areas.

A. Social Studies.

1. Specific objectives.
    a. To appreciate the help we receive from the people who take care of the city parks, picnic grounds, play areas, and public transportation.
    b. To realize that we cannot live without the help of many other people and that we must help others too.
    c. To learn about available places for good summer fun and the way to get there.
    d. To recognize the rights of others.
    e. To have respect for public and private property.
2. Development.
    a. Discussions concerning information gained through reading, viewing films, excursions, games, recordings, songs, etc. Pupils by groups or individually write stories about these things for experience charts and for review.
    b. Dramatizations using situations as they might be seen on a picnic ground or at the beach. Titles might be—"The Show-Off in the Swimming Pool" or "Careless Picnic Group at the Beach."
    c. Excursions to park, zoo, aquarium, or museum.
    d. Maps and pictures pertaining to the study.
    e. Films relating to the workers who help us and to places suitable for recreation, such as fishing, boating, or ball games.
    f. New songs relating to the unit.

B. Nutrition, Personal Health and Safety.

1. Objectives.
    a. To learn how to have an enjoyable summer with simple preparation.
    b. To learn to eat wisely in the summer; to prepare the right kinds of food for lunches and picnics.
    c. To learn social skills for summer happiness.
    d. To learn good grooming and correct costuming for summer outings and for home wear.
    e. To learn how to make some simple articles for summer use.
    f. To be familiar with the basic groups of foods.
    g. To learn simple safety rules for travel, picnics, and games.
    h. To learn simple first aid for insect bites, cuts, burns, and poison ivy.
    i. To prepare a picnic lunch.
2. Development.
    a. Reading for information on the topics. Give talks on manners, clothing, behavior, sanitation, grooming, health, safety, and table decorations.
    b. Dramatizing and actually practicing the following activities:
        (1) Prepare lunches using basic foods.
        (2) Set a picnic or luncheon table.
        (3) Learn how to serve and to be served at a picnic or luncheon.
        (4) Learn how to care for the skin, hair, nails, and teeth.
        (5) Learn how to care for clothes.
        (6) Learn how to avoid contagion at the beaches, swimming pools, and parks.
        (7) Learn what to do if stung by an insect, if cut, burned, or if brought in contact with poison ivy.
        (8) Learn how to be safe at a wiener roast.
        (9) Learn how to be safe when fishing or boating.

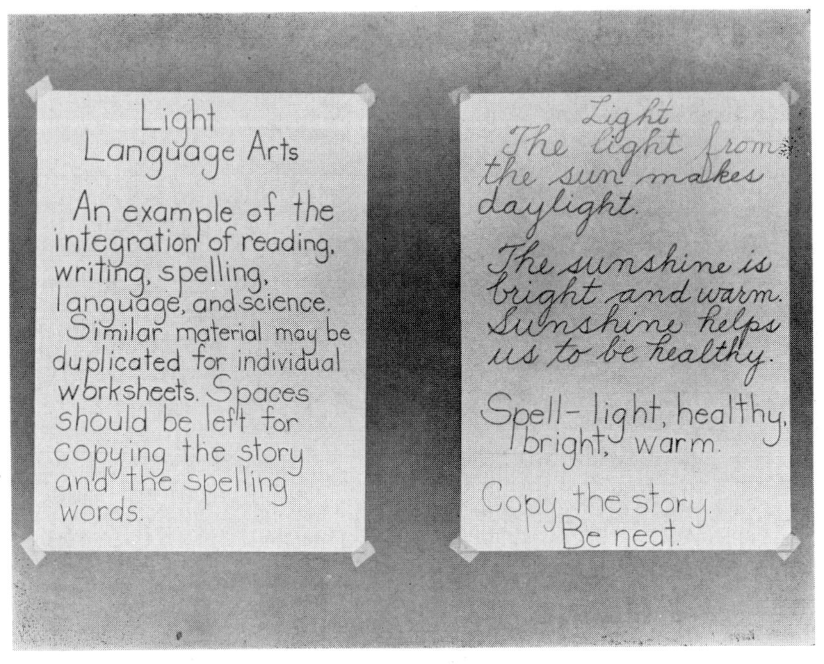

19. Worksheet–language arts.

(10) Know how to choose suitable games and how to play them.
(11) Be able to join in group singing or conversation.
(12) Make luncheon cloths, napkins, pottery.
(13) Make charts, posters, booklets about foods, health and safety.

c. Viewing films related to safety, personal health, and nutrition.

C. Language Arts.

1. Objectives.
   a. To learn skills in the tool subjects.
   b. To learn how to communicate with people through spoken and written language.
   c. To learn how to write simple letters, notes of thanks, and invitations.

d. To locate and read the different sections of the newspaper for information about foods, clothing, and types of recreation.
e. To develop desirable attitudes toward rewarding entertainment.
f. To learn how to locate places in the community through the use of the newspapers, telephone directory, and in answer to inquiry.
g. To read for information about community health, safety, transportaion, and the use of public facilities.
h. To listen to a story and be able to relate it to others for their entertainment.

2. Development.
   a. Use newspapers, telephone directory, books, catalog, library, experience charts, and all of the materials collected to gain information for the social studies area, and in other areas in the group's daily experiences. Direct the reading toward objectives listed under the areas of activity. Teach a sight vocabulary of words pertaining to safety. Present recordings of stories. Give individual help in mastering the ability to read. Discussion, conversations, and sharing experiences will develop the oral language ability.
   b. Teach writing as it is needed in such activities as the completion of menus, experience stories in the areas studied, stories of activities, letters of inquiry, notes of invitation and thanks. Give individual help in mastering the ability to write legibly.
   c. Limit spelling to words needed to carry on friendly correspondence and to make grocery or other lists. Select words from the pupils' daily work in the class. Give individual help to assist in learning to spell functional words.
   d. Develop Activities.
      (1) Discuss the following:
         (a) The places we are to visit.
         (b) The places other people have visited.

(c) The people who work to provide the equipment or materials we use for travel or play.
(d) The plans for the trip; when we go, how to get there, how to act on the trip, what to wear on the trip, where to eat, how much the trip will cost, and when to return home.
(e) The use of the telephone.

(2) Draw or paint pictures of the places we wish to visit or that we have visited.
(a) Writing stories of experiences we had during the summer.
(b) Making a booklet and a cover for the stories and the drawings.

(3) Dramatize experiences.

D. Arithmetic.

1. Objectives.
   a. To assist in developing independence in solving problems.
   b. To learn how to make change.
   c. To learn to tell time.
   d. To learn measurements of time, quantity, and distance.
   e. To become conscious of the time needed to go to different places and to return home.
   f. To develop the skills needed to solve simple problems encountered everyday in buying groceries, clothes, or recreation.
2. Development.
   a. Use functional problems prepared by the teacher in connection with foods, shop, science, nature study, and recreation.
   b. Drill on the needed skills in addition, subtraction, multiplication, and simple division.
   c. Use a sequential developmental pattern for presenting the needed skills.

d. Use films teaching the number concepts, number flash-cards, flannel board, rocks, buttons, spools or other objects for counters. Use the pegboard, abacus, scales, ruler, thermometer, measuring containers for liquids and bulky foods, play money, real money, and the telephone.

E. Music.
1. Objectives.
   a. To learn songs and dances for recreation.
   b. To attain social skills.
   c. To learn how to be socially acceptable.
   d. To learn good manners in a social situation.
   e. To learn to participate.
   f. To learn the rights of others.
   g. To learn to listen to music, to follow directions, and to take turns.
2. Development.
   a. Through songs.
   b. Through listening to recordings and other music.
   c. Through participation in many kinds of rhythm activities.

F. Science and Nature Study.
1. Objectives.
   a. To appreciate the beauty of summer time.
   b. To appreciate the value of sunshine to plant and animal life.
   c. To learn to care for the natural beauty of parks and recreation areas.
   d. To develop a feeling of responsibility and a desire to conserve the natural beauty and resources of our country.
   e. To learn about the insects, birds, and animals around the neighborhood and community in the summer.
   f. To learn about the different plants and flowers seen on picnics and excursions.
   h. To learn to look for the evening star, the Big Dipper, the North star, and the different phases of the moon.

i. To learn to ask questions about things seen so that they may become meaningful to the observer.

2. Development.
   a. Excursions, picnics, walks.
   b. Science books, story books, magazines, newspapers.
   c. Specimens.
   d. Stories written by children and read to the class.
   e. Drawings, modelings.
   f. Reports from observations or reading.
   g. Films and film-strips.
   h. Experiments.

G. Physical Education.

1. Objectives.
   a. To learn to enjoy healthful exercise for recreation.
   b. To appreciate sports for entertainment.
   c. To learn how to participate in some games for social acceptance as well as enjoyment.
   d. To learn fair play.
   e. To learn to respect the rights of others.
   f. To learn to take turns.
   g. To learn to appreciate the equipment and facilities used for recreation.
   h. To acquire good behavior patterns for group play.
   i. To learn individual responsibility for the proper use of public and private property and the importance of safety habits.
   j. To learn to make good use of leisure time.
   k. To learn the value of good health before participating in strenuous sports.

2. Development.
   a. Participate in recreation indoors and outdoors.
   b. Attend competitive games of various sports.
   c. Listen to radio and TV broadcasts of games.
   d. Make a scrapbook of pictures of athletic events.
   e. Read stories or view films about athletic events.

H. Industrial Arts.

1. Objectives.
    a. To learn the use and care of basic tools and materials.
    b. To acquire habits of safety and consideration for others.
    c. To learn the use of measurements and the value of accuracy.
2. Development.

    Make small articles, such as wooden coasters, hot-dish pads, small trays, and articles for recreational purposes.

I. Art

1. Objectives.
    a. To develop an appreciation of simple, orderly decoration.
    b. To develop behavior patterns suitable for working in groups.
    c. To learn to take turns.
    d. To learn to take measurements.
    e. To learn the use of color in decorating.
    f. To learn the value of accuracy in making an article.
    g. To learn the care of tools and equipment.
    h. To learn the value of materials, such as cloth, yarn, clay, or patterns.
    i. To learn skills connected with making different kinds of articles.
    j. To learn how to use textile paint in decorating articles.
    k. To learn how to make posters and booklet covers.
    l. To learn how to use clay and form small articles from it.
    m. To learn how to decorate the fired clay.
    n. To learn how to use patterns.
    o. To learn how to use the finished products.
2. Development.
    a. Present an opportunity to discuss picnics being planned or lunches to be given by the group. Ask for suggestions for table decorations and for the menus.

Call for suggestions for making articles that would contribute to a more attractive table.

b. Draw sketches of things that the children would like to make. Display the sketches and discuss their possibilities.
c. Plan for objects that are functional.
d. See that each child will have a satisfying experience.
e. Decide on one type of work, such as clay modeling, for all to use for the first project.

IV. Presentation

A. Discuss with the children the many ways they may have fun during vacation in the summer. List the suggestions given by the children: trips to the beach; fishing; boating; picnics; excursions; visits to the park or zoo; backyard picnics; swimming; traveling; playing games; listening to music; gardening; playing with pets; going to ball games or playing ball.
B. Make charts of the suggestions given by the pupils.
C. Guide the class in deciding on a question for the next lesson and in looking for materials. The teacher makes the experience charts, sentence strips, flash cards, and worksheets for class reading, writing, and spelling. She should follow through on the class questions, and, as new ideas are expressed, the entire core unit will grow. The watchful teacher will be able to guide the suggestions into useful channels in the different areas of the plan.

V. Evaluation

Benefits derived by the class from the study of the unit included:

A. A more wholesome attitude toward friends and neighbors.
B. A better understanding of what is expected of either a spectator or a participant in various forms of recreation and entertainment.
C. A better appreciation of the facilities offered for our pleasure in summer.
D. A feeling of part ownership in community recreation facilities, with attendant feelings of responsibility for their care and proper use.

E. Increased knowledge of plant, animal, and insect life.
F. An increased feeling of self-respect.
G. Development of greater self-reliance and independence.
H. Interest in possible future employment and economic independence.
I. Increased skill in tool subjects and in the functional areas leading toward vocational training.
J. Stimulation of better oral and written language.
K. More legible writing.
L. Improved spelling ability.
M. Increased interest in art and crafts.
N. Increased interest in reading.
O. Increased ability to sing, play games, and use basic skills.
P. Increased understanding of useful words.

BIBLIOGRAPHY

1. Ackley, Edith Flack: *Dolls to Make for Fun and Profit.* New York, J. B. Lippincott, 1951. (5-8)
2. Anderson, Clarence W.: *Afraid to Ride.* New York, Macmillan Company, 1957.
3. Anderson, Clarence W.: *Blaze and Thunderbolt.* New York, Macmillan Company, 1955.
4. Anderson, Clarence W.: *Pony for Three.* New York, Macmillan Company, 1958.
5. Association for Childhood Education: *Sung Under the Silver Umbrella.* New York, Macmillan Company, 1945.
6. Association for Childhood Education: *Told Under Spacious Skies.* New York, Macmillan Company, 1952.
7. Aulaire, Ingri d' and Aulaire, Edgar Parin: *Animals Everywhere.* Garden City, New York, Doubleday, 1954. (k-3) Animal Stories.
8. Beim, Jerrold: *Tim and the Tool Chest.* New York, Morrow and Company, 1951. (1-3)
9. Beim, Jerrold: *Time for Gym.* New York, Morrow and Company, 1957. (1-3)
10. Blough, Glenn O.: *After the Sun Goes Down.* New York, (Whittlesey House) McGraw-Hill Book Company, 1956.

11. Blough, Glenn O.: *Wait for the Sunshine.* New York, (Whittlesey House) McGraw-Hill Book Company, 1954. (2-4) Seasons and growing things, illustrated.
12. Blough, Glenn O.: *Who Lives in This House?* New York, (Whittlesey House) McGraw-Hill Book Company, 1957.
13. Bronson, Wilfred S.: *The Grasshopper Book.* New York, Harcourt, Brace and Company, 1943.
14. Bronson, Wilfred S.: *Polliwoggle's Progress.* New York, Harcourt, Brace and Company, 1949.
15. Browne, Georgiana K.: *Look and See.* Los Angeles, Melmont Publishers, Inc., 1958.
16. Buck, Margaret Waring: *In Ponds and Streams.* Nashville, Abingdon Press, 1955.
17. Buck, Margaret Waring: *In Woods and Fields.* New York, Abingdon-Cokesbury Press, 1950.
18. Buck, Margaret Waring: *In Yards and Gardens.* New York, Abingdon-Cokesbury Press, 1952.
19. Carlson, Bernice Wells: *Act It Out.* New York, Abingdon Press, 1956. Children's plays.
20. Carlson, Bernice Wells: *Fun for One or Two.* New York, Abingdon-Cokesbury Press, 1954 (3-6) Collection of indoor activities.
21. Carlson, Bernice Wells: *Make It and Use It.* New York, Abingdon Press, 1958. Handicrafts for boys and girls.
22. Chapman, Jane A.: *Girl's Book of Sewing.* New York, Greenberg, 1952. (4-9)
23. Clapper Publishing Company, Incorporated: *How to Make Sock Toys, Three Hundred Sixty-Five Easy Scrapcraft Ideas.* Park Ridge, Illinois, Clapper Publishing Company, Incorporated, 1959.
24. Cormack, Maribelle: *First Book of Trees.* F. Watts, 1951. (3-7)
25. DeLeeuw, Adele Louise: *It's Fun to Cook.* New York, Macmillan Company, 1952. (6-9)
26. Duvoisin, Roger Antoine: *Two Lonely Ducks.* New York, Knopf, 1955. (k-1) Counting book.
27. Elting, Mary: *First Book of Firemen.* (Benjamin Brewster, pseud.) New York, F. Watts, 1951. (1-4)
28. Elting, Mary: *Ships at Work.* Garden City, New York, Garden City Books, 1953.
29. Encyclopaedia Britannica Picture Story Booklets: Chicago, Encyclopaedia Britannica Press.

30. Frasier, George W., and Dolman, Helen: The Scientific Living Series, *Sunshine and Rain,* rev. ed., *Winter Comes and Goes,* rev. ed., *The How and Why Club,* rev. ed., Syracuse, New York, L. W. Singer and Company, 1952.
31. Frissell, Bernice O., and Friebele, Mary L.: *Fun At the Playground,* reprint. New York, Macmillan Company, 1950.
32. Frissell, Bernice O.: *Fun in Swimming.* New York, Macmillan Company, 1946.
33. Gaul, Albro T.: *Picture Book of Insects.* New York, Lothrop, Lee and Shephard Company, 1943.
34. Gaul, Albro T.: *The Pond Book.* New York, Coward-McCann, 1955.
35. Hanna, Paul Robert and Kohn, Clyde F.: *Cross Country.* Chicago, Scott, Foresman and Company, 1950.
36. Heal, Edith: *First Book of America.* New York, F. Watts, 1952. (3-5) The story of freedom, of the ideas, and of the men who led the way and shaped our country's growth.
37. Huntington, Harriet E.: *Let's Go to the Brook.* Garden City, New York, Doubleday, 1952. (1-3)
38. Huntington, Harriet E.: *Praying Mantis.* Garden City, New York, Doubleday, 1957.
39. Hylander, C. J.: *Out of Doors in Spring.* New York, Macmillan Company, 1950.
40. Hylander, C. J.: *Out of Doors in Summer.* New York, Macmillan Company, 1950.
41. Knox, Warren William: *The Wonderworld of Science.* New York, Charles Scribner's Sons, 1950.
42. Limbach, Russell T.: *American Trees.* New York, Random House, 1942.
43. Marcher, Marion W.: *Monarch Butterfly.* New York, Holiday, 1954. (1-4) Life cycle of butterfly.
44. Matschat, Cecile Hulse: *American Butterflies and Moths.* New York, Random House, 1942.
45. McClintock, Marshall: *Let's Learn the Flowers.* New York, Chanticleer Press, 1948.
46. McClintock, Marshall: *Leaf, Fruit, and Flower.* New York, Chanticleer Press, 1948. Nature primer.
47. McClung, Robert M.: *Green Darner.* New York, Morrow and Company, 1956. Story of a dragonfly.

48. McClung, Robert M.: *Sphinx.* New York, Morrow and Company, 1949.
49. McClung, Robert M.: *Stripe.* New York, Morrow and Company, 1951. Story of a chipmunk.
50. McClung, Robert M.: *Tiger.* New York, Morrow and Company, 1953. (1-3) Story of a swallowtail butterfly.
51. McGregor, Ellen: *Tommy and the Telephone.* Chicago, Albert Whitman and Company, 1950.
52. McIntire, Alta: *Billy Goes to School.* Chicago, Follett Publishing Company, 1949.
53. McKee, Paul and Harrison, M. Lucile: Reading for Meaning Series, *With Jack and Janet, Up and Away, On We Go, Looking Ahead,* rev. eds., Chicago, Houghton Mifflin Company, 1957.
54. Morrow, Betty: *See Up the Mountain.* New York, Harper and Brothers, 1958.
55. Norling, Josephine (Stearns) and Norling, Earnest Ralph: *First Book of Water.* New York, F. Watts, 1952. (2-4) The many roles of water.
56. Parker, Bertha Morris: *Basic Science Education Series.* Evanston, Illinois, Row, Peterson and Company, 1941-1952. A series of booklets on many science and nature subjects.
57. Parker, Bertha Morris: *The Golden Book of Science.* New York, Simon and Schuster, 1956.
58. Patch, Edith M.: *Holiday Meadows,* New York, Macmillan Company, 1945.
59. Pistorius, Anna: *What Bird Is It?* 1945; *What Animal Is It?* 1947; *What Butterfly Is It?* 1949; *What Wildflower Is It?* 1950; *What Tree Is It?* 1955. Chicago, Wilcox and Follett Publishing Company. (3-5)
60. Pistorius, Anna: *What Dinosaur Is It?* Chicago, Follett Publishing Company, 1958.
61. Pistorius, Anna: *What Dog Is It?* Chicago, Wilcox and Follett Publishing Company, 1951.
62. Pondendorf, Illa: *True Book of Pets,* 1954; *True Book of Science Experiments,* 1954; *True Book of Weeds and Wild Flowers,* 1955. Chicago, Children's Press. (1-4)
63. Reed, William Maxwell: *Patterns in the Sky.* New York, Morrow and Company, 1951. (5-8) Maps, and the story of the constellations.

64. Rogers, Frances and Beard, Alice: *The Birthday of a Nation.* New York, J. B. Lippincott, 1945.

65. Rogers, Frances: *Fire Engine Boy.* New York, J. B. Lippincott, 1953.

66. Rogers, Frances: *Lens Magic. Philadelphia,* J. B. Lippincott, 1957.

67. Schlein, Miriam: *How Do You Travel?* Nashville, Tennessee; Abingdon Press, 1954.

68. Schneider, Herman and Schneider, Nina: *You Among the Stars.* New York, W. R. Scott, 1951. (3-5)

69. Schwartz, Julius: *It's Fun to Know Why.* New York, (Whittlesey House) McGraw-Hill Book Company, 1952. (4-7) Experiments with things around us.

70. Seignobosc, Francoise: *Springtime for Jeanne-Marie.* New York, Charles Scribner's Sons, 1955. (k-1)

71. Selsam, Millicent E.: *Nature Detective.* New York, W. R. Scott, 1958.

72. Selsam, Millicent E.: *Seeds and More Seeds.* New York, Harper and Brothers, 1959.

73. Shannon, Terry: *Where Animals Live.* Chicago, Albert Whitman and Company, 1958.

74. Smith, J. Russell, and others: *Our Neighbors at Home.* Philadelphia, John C. Winston Company, 1952.

75. Smith, Marie Elizabeth: Social Learning Readers, *Bill's Story of the Wholesale Produce Market, Bob's Story of the Retail Market, Joe's Story of the Airport, Mother's Story of Dairying.* New York, Charles Scribner's Sons, 1951.

76. Tibbets, Albert B.: *First Book of Bees.* F. Watts, 1952. (3-5) Story of how bees live in communities.

77. Tresselt, Alvin: *Johnny Mapleleaf.* New York, Lothrop, Lee and Shephard Company, 1948.

78. Tresselt, Alvin: *I Saw the Sea Come In.* New York, Lothrop, Lee and Shephard Company. 1954. (k-1) A boy explores the beach on foggy morning and finds children's kind of treasures. He saw the tide come in while he was alone. When the sun came out, other people came to the beach.

79. Tresselt, Alvin: *The Rabbit Story.* New York, Lothrop, Lee and Shephard, 1957.

80. Warner, Gertrude Chandler: *The Box Car Children.* Chicago, Scott, Foresman and Company, 1942. (3-4) Four children who are orphans run away from an imaginary evil grandfather. They live in a box car and have many adventures. They get to know the grandfather and love him before they discover he is the man they ran away from.
81. Watson, Jane Werner: *Wonders of Nature.* New York, Golden Press, 1958.
82. Wilcox, Charlotte E., McCall, Edith S., and Bolton, William, M. D., Health Action Series, *Come On* (Grade 1), *Here We Go* (Grade 2), *Step Lively* (Grade 3). Chicago, Beckley-Cardy Company, 1956.
83. Willcockson, Mary: Winston's Primary Social Studies Series, *Nancy's World,* 1949; *Tom's Town,* 1950; *Other Places,* 1950. Philadelphia, John C. Winston Company.
84. Williamson, Margaret: *First Book of Birds.* New York, F. Watts, 1951. (2-6)
85. Wyler, Rose: *The First Book of Weather.* New York, F. Watts, 1956.
86. Wyler, Rose: *Planet Earth.* New York, H. Schuman, 1952.
87. Zarchy, Harry: *Creative Hobbies.* New York, Knopf, 1953.
88. Zarchy, Harry: *Leathercraft.* New York, Knopf, 1953.
89. Zarchy, Harry: *Let's Make More Things.* New York, Knopf, 1943.
90. Zarchy, Harry: *Model Railroading.* New York, Knopf, 1955.
91. Zarchy, Harry: *Stamp Collector's Guide.* New York, Knopf, 1956.
92. Zarchy, Harry: *Woodworking.* New York, Knopf, 1952. (3-5) A father and son activity book.
93. Zim, Herbert S.: *Comets.* New York, Morrow and Company, 1957.
94. Zim, Herbert S.: *Dinosaurs.* New York, Morrow and Company, 1954.
95. Zim, Herbert S.: *Fishes.* New York, Simon and Schuster, 1956.
96. Zim, Herbert S.: *Frogs and Toads.* New York, Morrow and Company, 1950.
97. Zim, Herbert S.: *Lightning and Thunder.* New York, Morrow and Company, 1952. (4-7)
98. Zim, Herbert S., and Baker, Robert Horace: *Stars.* New York, Simon and Schuster, 1951. (3-5)
99. Zim, Herbert S.: *The Sun.* New York, Morrow and Company, 1953. (3-6)

20. Materials for a unit on "The Weather."

100. Zim, Herbert S.: *What's Inside of Plants?* 1952; (2-5) *What's Inside of Animals?* 1953; (2-4) *What's Inside of Me?* 1952; (2-5) New York, Morrow and Company.

THE WEATHER

I. Purpose

To assist the children in developing an awareness and understanding of some facts about the weather; to be able to discuss the weather with others regarding the natural phenomena of clouds, rain, and thunder storms; and to be able, by referring to forecasts, to dress properly and to stay well and healthy.

II. Objectives

A. To understand what clouds are and how they are formed.
B. To understand the cause of rain and its importance to us.
C. To know what to wear in the rain.
D. To know where to seek protection during thunder storms and tornadoes.
E. To know how to read the thermometer.

III. Integration

A. Arithmetic.

1. Learned how to read the thermometer.
2. Keep a chart of daily weather and temperature.
3. Make thermometers of paper for recording and practicing reading of temperatures.
4. Use measuring and numbering for thermometers.

B. Health and Safety.

1. Discuss lightning, thunder, and tornadoes.
   a. Causes
   b. Proper precautions for safety and health.
2. Discuss protection of the body when out in severe weather.

C. Language Arts.

1. Listen to weather reports on the radio or T-V.
2. Read weather reports.
3. Read stories about the weather.
4. Discuss these reports in class.
5. Write stories about personal experiences in various kinds of weather.
6. Read these stories to the group.
7. Learn new words.
8. Discuss effects of weather on customs and culture of people.

IV. Materials and Methods

A. Present experiments that help explain the phenomena of rain, snow, fog, wind, and storms.

B. Keep daily weather and temperature charts.

C. Show different kinds of thermometers, such as weather, candy, fever, and oven.

D. Present experiment showing how the thermometer works.

E. Make replicas of thermometers for daily seat work. Read the real thermometer several times daily and change the replicas to match. Make a large replica of the thermometer for the bulletin board.

F. Make scrap books or booklets.

V. Presentation

A. The daily lesson plans.

1. Lesson one.

   Prepare a large thermometer of light weight cardboard. Mark the degrees for temperature plainly. Thread a narrow red ribbon through a slot at the lower end and fasten it to a white ribbon coming down from the slot at the top. After an explanation to the class place it on the bulletin board. Show other kinds of thermometers to the children and explain their uses.

2. Lesson two.

   The teacher should help the children make small thermometers similar to the large one on the bulletin board. Keep these in the scrap books or with the stories about the weather for a special booklet.

3. Lesson three.

   a. Provide a calendar form for the children to keep a daily record of the weather and temperature. Show them how to use the form and write the record for that day. Keep these with the other weather stories and materials.

   b. Change the temperature daily on the children's play thermometers so that they will become aware of the changing weather.

   c. Appoint a helper to have charge of the real thermometer and adjust the one on the bulletin board daily.

   d. Write a short story on the chalkboard about the weather to be copied by the children for their story booklets.

   e. Write a list of new words on the chalkboard for the children to copy and learn.

   f. Assign these words according to ability for spelling words.

4. Lesson four.

   a. Take the group to the library. Look for information about the weather.

   b. Check out books and materials for further study and for reports.

5. Lesson fiive.
   a. Children make oral reports on materials they found at the library.
   b. Make a list of words from the reports for spelling and for sight recognition.
   c. Use a flashcard drill for words on the previous list.
6. Lesson six.
   a. Show a film about the weather.
   b. Hear reports from the class about the film.
   c. Add new words to the spelling list.
   d. Hear spelling of words on previous list.
7. Lesson seven.
   a. Write on the chalkboard the story that the group dictates, listing things they have learned about the weather.
   b. Read this story to the class and have the puplis read it.
   c. Select words for spelling list.
   d. Have pupils copy this story for their booklets.
   e. Spell the words from lesson six.
8. Lesson eight.
   a. Tell stories about the weather.
   b. Write stories about the weather.
   c. Help the pupils with spelling words needed for their stories.
   d. Put stories into booklets.
   e. Add new words to spelling list.
9. Lesson nine.
   a. Read or tell an interesting story to the group about some true or fictitious event caused by weather conditions.
   b. Write on the chalkboard a story as it is dictated by the class.
   c. List new words for spelling.
   d. Review all flashcards for new vocabulary from lesson one through the present lesson.

10. Lesson ten.
    a. Present an experiment showing how the thermometer works.
    b. Make a chart showing the steps in the experiment and the way the thermometer works.
    c. Have the pupils copy this chart.
    d. Add new words to spelling list.
    e. Spell the words from the previous list.
11. Lesson eleven.
    a. Discuss the causes of rain, fog, snow, wind, and storms.
    b. Show a film demonstrating these things, or have pictures available to illustrate the discussion.
    c. Add new words to the spelling and vocabulary list.
    d. Spell the words from the previous list.
12. Lesson 12.
    a. Read stories about rain, thunder, lightning, and other storms.
    b. Discuss safety and health precautions.
    c. Have the class give stories about things they have learned concerning the weather.
    d. Have the class write the stories for their booklets.
    e. Add new spelling words to the list.
    f. Spell the words from lesson eleven.
13. Lesson thirteen.
    a. Present experiment showing how rain is caused by warm, moist air meeting cool air.
    b. Make a chart showing the steps in the experiment.
    c. Present simple water barometer and explain how it works.
    d. Copy this chart for the scrapbooks or booklets.
    e. Add new words to spelling and vocabulary lists.
    f. Spell the words from the previous lesson.
14. Lesson fourteen.
    a. Discuss proper clothing to wear in various kinds of weather.
    b. Discuss other care of the body for health at different times of the year.

c. Review safety and health rules for weather and storms.
d. Try to relieve fears about thunder storms.
e. Copy on the chalkboard as the class dictates it a story about health and safety during storms.
f. Have the class copy the story for their booklets.

15. Lesson fifteen.
   a. Collect all of the drawings and stories from each child.
   b. Use drawings and stories for booklets.
   c. Have the children assist in assembling the booklets.
   d. Have each child select one of his own stories and read it to the group.
   e. Evaluate the unit and list the outcomes.
   f. Note if the class has an interest in some phase of the unit that would warrant further study. For example, if the group is interested in clouds, a short series of lessons about that topic may be beneficial. Use the same general outline—but simplify it.

VI. Bibliography

List the materials that were used in presenting this unit.

CLOUDS

I. Purpose

To learn more about the causes of rain, snow, and other weather conditions.

II. Objectives

To learn what causes different kinds of clouds and what the different kinds of clouds mean to the man on the ground and to the man in the air.

III. Integration

A. Arithmetic.

Present material about distances; height of clouds from the ground; size of clouds; amounts of rainfall and snow; velocity of the wind; how fast storms travel; size of hail stones.

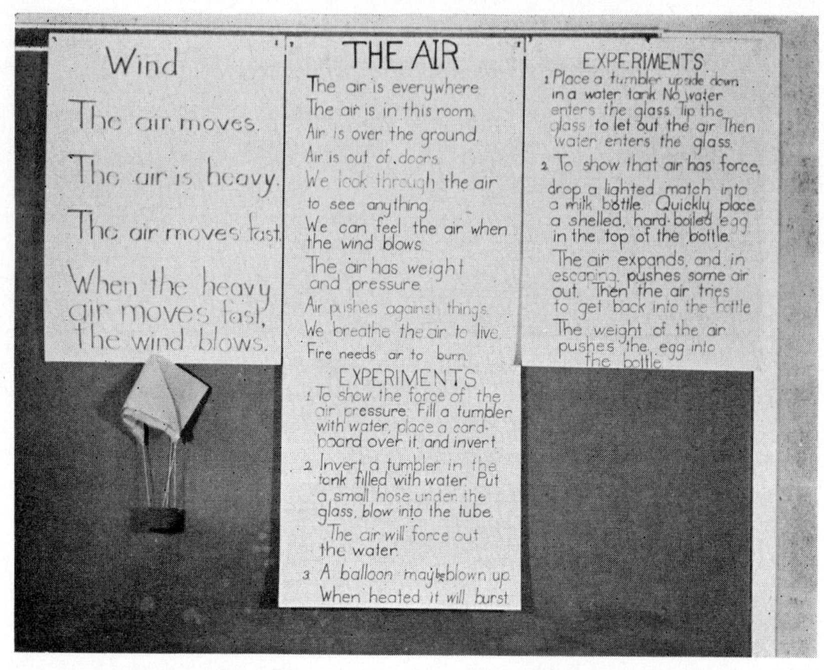

21. Experience charts about the air.

B. Language Arts.

Direct oral and written language exercises; reading for information and pleasure; spelling new words; writing for legibility.

C. Art.

Direct drawing and painting of cloud formations.

IV. Materials

Use films, pictures, and the sky.

V. Activities

A. Locate pictures for the bulletin board.

B. Watch the sky for cloud formations.

C. Read weather reports.

D. Field trip to airport; discuss weather with the manager; the effect of weather on flying; difficulty of landing in a high wind.

E. Make weather vanes.
F. Make experience charts.
G. View films or other audio-visual media.

VI. Presentation

A. The lesson plans.
1. Lesson one.
a. Discuss clouds in general. Get a story from the group showing what they know about clouds.
b. Compile a listof things the pupils want to know about the clouds.
c. Direct the children to copy the story and the list in their note books.
d. List new words for spelling.
2. Lesson two.
a. Form committees to look for materials about clouds.
b. Read stories and show pictures about clouds to the group.
c. Spell words from lesson one list.
d. Put new spelling words on list.
e. Make flash cards and have word drill.
3. Lesson three.
a. Hear committee reports.
b. Check the list of questions and assign new questions to the committees.
c. Write the answers to questions on the chalkboard for the pupils to copy for their writing lesson.
e. Spell the words on the list and add new words.
4. Lesson four.
a. Hear committee reports.
b. Make a weather vane and a rain gauge.
c. Spell the words assigned and add new words to the list.
5. Lesson five.
a. Take trip to the airport.
b. Show a film about clouds.
c. Discuss the trip and film.

d. Make a class story about the trip and the scenes from the film.
e. Copy the story for the scrap book.
f. Spell the words from the list and add new words.
g. Prepare stories and drawings for the booklet.

VII. Outcomes

Evaluate the results of the study.

VIII. Bibliography

Let the children prepare their own list of source materials.

6

WRITING

THE OBJECTIVES IN TEACHING WRITING

THE objective in teaching the mentally retarded child to write is to help him achieve legibility for communication. This involves neatness, attention to letter size, spacing, smooth forms, and, in cursive writing, the proper joining of the letters to form words.

IMPORTANCE OF ESTABLISHING CORRECT HABITS

Writing is one subject that depends largely upon habit for its efficient use. Writing, a sensori-motor skill, is learned by repetition. The movements of the arms and fingers are stimulated by visual, auditory, or mental images. Children should write with large movements until they are able to control and integrate their muscular coordination. This usually occurs when the child is about seven or eight years of age.

After continued practice has made the skill automatic, it becomes a tool for better communication. When a mentally retarded child has learned to write, he has more status with other children. His acquired ability will give him self-confidence and a better social standing with adults.

VALUE OF WRITING ONE'S NAME

Everyone needs to know how to write his name, write letters and notes to relatives and friends, make a list of materials or groceries, keep simple records, fill out applications, or write a receipt. The child wants to label his belongings and his drawings,

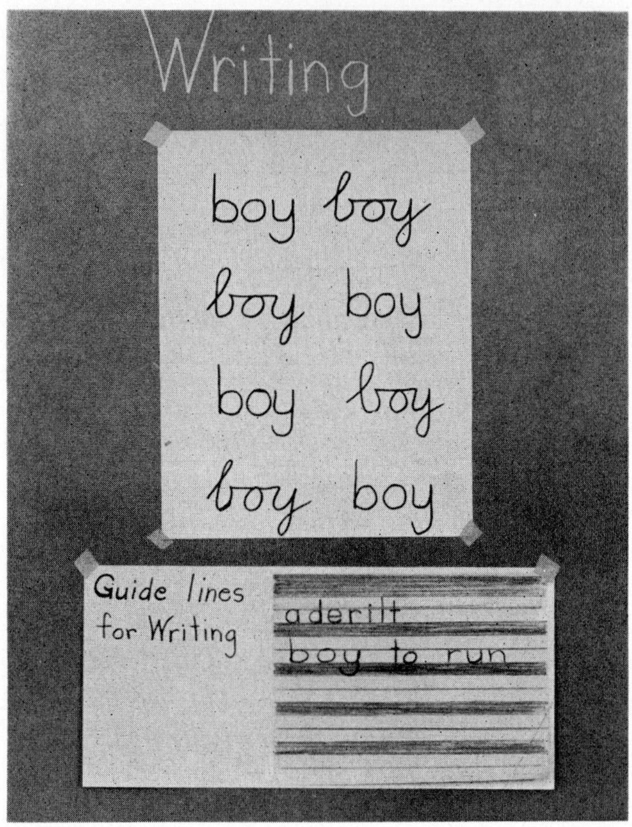

22. Illustration for teaching spacing in writing and a practice sheet for cursive writing.

copy a story to take home to mother, or write a note of invitation to a school play. As these needs appear, the child's interest is stimulated and motivation is accelerated.

INTRODUCING OF CURSIVE WRITING

In most schools the child is introduced first to manuscript writing and later is taught to change over to the cursive letter forms. The educable mentally retarded child could profit by being taught cursive instead of manuscript writing, as this would help him to visualize the word as a unit. The child who uses the manuscript form has a strong tendency to write the words together without spacing.

Some children who have been taught the manuscript form seem unable to learn to use script. Many teachers feel that, as long as the educable mentally retarded are proficient in manuscript writing, there is no need to change. Even those who are able to change from manuscript to the cursive form are seldom ready for it before they are twelve years of age or have achieved third grade academic ability.

The child can learn to use script to *draw* his name at an early age. This skill satisfies his family and friends and prepares him for signing legal documents. However, he should learn to read and to write script if possible, for he will want to read letters and notes from friends.

When the child has some muscular coordination, he should be shown how to form the letters correctly. This may be done as a group or individually. He should have pages for practice in making the script forms of the letters. Here, as in manuscript writing, a device that is of assistance to the busy teacher is to prepare complete sheets of each letter in small and in capital forms for tracing. The use of different colors for each repetition of a word or letter compels the child to observe when a form is completed.

Tracing paper may be clipped to the cards or pages and the child shown how to trace over the copy. He may be given five or six sheets of tracing paper so that he can change the used sheet for a fresh one. The teacher should check him frequently to see if he is making the letter forms correctly. It may be necessary to hold his hand and to help him trace until he gains confidence enough to work alone. He should hand all of the practice sheets back to the teacher to be checked.

Importance of Teacher Proficiency. The teacher herself should practice letter formation until she is in complete command of the process before attempting to teach it to the mentally retarded. There are many good systems that may be studied.

MANUSCRIPT WRITING

Although the child should have good posture for any writing, the posture for manuscript writing is slightly different from that for script. The child should sit straight at the desk with feet flat on the floor. His arms should rest on the desk. The paper should

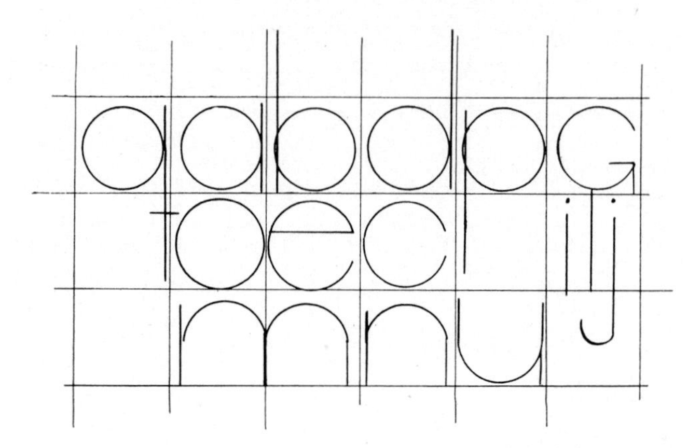

23. Presenting manuscript writing to the children.

be vertical to the body. The soft lead pencil should be held comfortably between thumb and fingers. Since the mentally retarded child has a tendency to slump in his seat, special attention must be given to retaining good writing posture. The teacher should walk about the room and lightly touch the slouched child on the back to remind him to sit properly.

The half-inch squared paper will be a helpful aid to the child if he has difficulty in spacing, or in keeping the letters within a good range of size.

Letters like *l, i,* and *j,* that are narrow, take up half a space. When they are used together in a word, as in *lilt,* at least a third of space should be left around each letter.

There are two wide letters, *M* and *W*. In the capital forms, they take up as much space as a round letter, but the small case forms of these same letters take one and one-half to two spaces, depending upon the system being taught. Most systems of manuscript writing use the *M* with the straight sides and the *W* with the flared sides. This device also asssists the mentally retarded child to remember which is an *M* or a *W*.

In teaching the tall letters, leave plenty of space between the lines so that the letters do not overlap. All of the letters should be formed simply and precisely, without curls or decorations which confuse the children.

The teacher should explain to the child that he must keep the

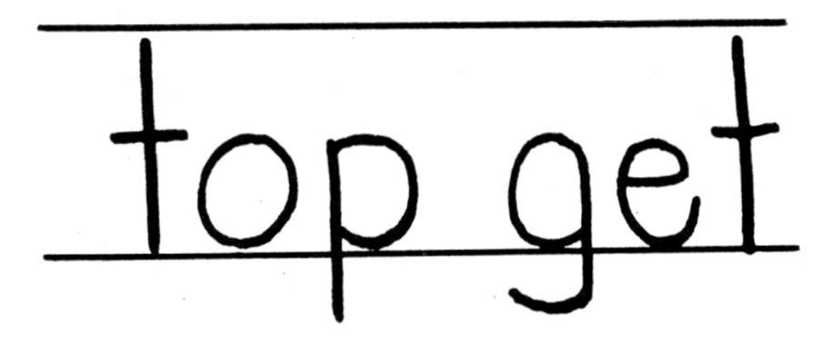

24. Spacing for tall letters.

letters tall and straight above the line or long below the line so that they are easily distinguished from the short letters. It is better to skip a line on the paper in order that all of the letters will be formed perfectly.

The round letters are made close together as in the words *soon, see* and *bead.* The spacing is important for neat writing. Watchfulness at the early stage will prevent bad letter formation and sloppy writing.

PRESENTATION OF THE FIRST MANUSCRIPT WRITING LESSON

Use of the Chalkboard. The teacher may find the following directions helpful:

1. Use a music liner to draw lines on the chalkboard. Omit the chalk from the clamps numbered two and four. Have the lines drawn before the class assembles. Use soft chalk to form the letters, because it makes a broad stroke that is easy to read.

2. Present all of the lower case forms first. These forms are based on a circle and a straight line.

Chalkboard Practice. Children who have never written will make faster progress by regular practice at the chalkboard than by starting with pencil and paper at their seats. This type of practice uses the large arm and shoulder muscles and produces a kinesthetic feeling for the form of the letters.

Desk Practice. After the child has practiced at the chalkboard for a time, the teacher should show him how to practice with paper and pencil at his desk. One method of helping the child achieve success is described below. Here are directions for the teacher to follow.

1. Prepare the chalkboard with lines before the class assembles.

2. Prepare a cardboard disk that will fit between the lines on the board. Have a foot ruler and chalk at the chalkboard.

3. Have a supply of writing paper and medium-soft lead pencils ready to distribute. The practice paper should have wide-spaced lines with light guide lines between the heavy base lines. These base lines may be emphasized with a heavy line of crayon.

4. For each child, have a six-inch ruler and disk the right size to fit between the lines of the writing paper.

5. Stand in front of the group and see that every child has his desk cleared and is paying attention. Talk to the children about what they are going to see you do and what they will be doing themselves very soon.

Use simple directions like these: "Keep watching me. See this circle. See this chalk. I am going to draw an *O*. Watch me. I will make another *O*. Draw around the disk from the top down on the left side and then up on the right. See, I draw around this way."

6. Pass the practice paper, pencils, rulers, and disks. Play money of the nickel or dime size is excellent for disks. Say "Now you may try to make an *O*. Place the paper straight in front of you. Put both feet on the floor. Sit up straight. Raise your arms and let them drop on the desk beside the paper. Pick up the pencil in the hand you use for drawing pictures. Pick up the disk in the other hand. Lay the disk on the paper *between* the heavy blue lines."

"Now you may try. Some of you know how to do this, but since it is fun to do, we will all draw *O* at the same time."

7. Walk about the group, checking and showing how to place the disks. See that the children all understand what is meant by *between*. Continue directing the children: "All together, draw around the disk." Hold the children's hands and guide them to form the letter correctly. Repeat many times, "go down and around and up."

8. Try to make a rhythm of the exercise as you repeat, "*O*. Go down on the left side, around and up to the top. *O*. Pick up the disk. Lay it down. Draw around the disk. Go down on the left side. *O*. Pick up the disk. *O*. Lay down the disk. Look to see if the disk is between the lines."

Remind the children to keep a nice space between the letters. Unless they have guidance on spacing, all of the letters will be too close together.

After several rows have been made by specific direction, go about, guiding hands and offering praise as the next row of *O's* is being made without direction. Those who are able to do so may now make a row of *O's*, using the narrower space and no disks for guides. The other children continue using the disks.

When a row is completed, each pupil should lay down the disk and pencil and sit straight to indicate that he is ready to have his work checked.

Let those children whose letters are neat and well shaped and who have had writing experience proceed with copying words from a chart which you have prepared. These should be simple words beginning with *O* or having *O* in them. The other children continue to draw the *O*. Let them whisper, "O, O," as they form the letters.

Repeat the procedure for many, many lessons. There are some children who will need other reinforcements to help the memory process.

TRACING IN CLAY

Use tracing in clay as another method to aid the child to learn the letters' forms. Since this substance offers resistance to the muscles, it slows down the writing process so that the child can remember what he is doing.

25. The Clay Pan.

Directions for Making a Clay Pan for Tracing. Select an ordinary tin or aluminum cookie pan, about 12 x 18 inches, with very low sides or rims. A pound or two of an oil base plastic clay is a good medium for the writing mixture. Smooth this evenly over the bottom of the pan.

Use an orange stick or large wooden skewer to trace a word or letter lightly on the clay. Give the stylus to a child and show him how to trace while he repeats the letter or word. Most children enjoy this type of repetition. After the child has made a deep mark to the bottom of the pan, allow him to smooth out the clay and start a new copy.

Presentation of a. Use the chalkboard, the liner, and the disk for the letter form of *a* the same as in presenting *O*. Direct the children: "Today we will learn to make the letter that says *a*, giving the short sound. First we will make an *o*. Then take the ruler in your left hand and put it on the right side of the *o*. Draw a little line from the line on your writing paper at the top of the *o*, right against the o. Draw down to the bottom line on the paper that the *o* sits on. Lift the ruler. That is an *a*."

Proceed with the same instructions as for teaching *O*. Practice an *a* and *o* for several days; then follow with the round lower case letters.

Presentation of the Tall Letter d. To introduce the letter *d*, proceed in the same manner as for *a*, but explain and show that *d* has a tall line on the right side. The tall line must reach away up to the next line on the writing paper above the top of the *a*.

If possible, give some distinguishing characteristic to each letter so that the child will have a peg upon which to hang the letter in his memory. Proceed with the presentation of the rest of the letters of the alphabet using the disk and ruler to demonstrate their correct forms.

KINESTHETIC TRAINING

As another means of helping the child remember the letters, paste cutouts of the letters on small cards made from various materials. Since a rough surface will be remembered more easily than a very smooth one, fine sandpaper is excellent for this purpose. Let the child lightly trace over the outline with his forefinger.

On cardboard make another set of letters. Cut out the letter to form a stencil on the cardboard which the child may block out with his pencil. When he lifts the card, the heavy black letter remains in a true form.

There are many commercial materials available, such as stencils, plastic letters, letters for flannel boards, and magnetic letters for steel boards.

Give the child with a muscular involvement a large, very soft pencil. Wrap the center of the pencil with tape, or push a soft rubber ball onto the pencil to aid in grasping it more efficiently.

As the children attempt to write the letters, go about the group and help them. Show them how to hold the pencil and how to place the ruler vertically across the lines on the writing paper to make the stems of the letters. Explain the directions by showing them again with their rulers and disks what is meant by "Draw straight up and down," or "Draw around the disk."

Be patient! *Repeat* and *show*, and *help* the child *to do*.

Regardless of the order in which you decide to present the letters, be consistent in presenting their formation. Use the circle and the straight line in teaching manuscript letter forms; watch both the spacing of the letters and the spacing between the words to avoid crowding on the lines.

Demonstrate on the chalkboard each day the lesson that is to be taught. The children learn much from watching the writing process on the board.

CONSONANTS

Follow the basic reading series being used by the group in presenting the initial consonants in sequence. In teaching writing, always use the name of the consonant instead of its sound. Introduce the beginning consonant sound by using the words that are prepared for practice writing. In teaching the letter *d,* pronounce words from the list, such as dog, do, and day.

A child who is having trouble remembering where to start a new row of writing may use heavily blocked out areas above and below the lines to show the space in which he is to write.

After the pupils complete the small letters, start the capital letters. Proceed in the same manner as in presenting the lower case letters. Start with the round letters and the vowels and then follow later with the consonants.

If the children are not producing good letter formation, slow down the procedure and review until neat legible copy is obtained. Begin to emphasis the names of the letters and to try for rapid recognition.

Continue with the short lists of words, beginning with the letter being taught for practice writing. Add a short sentence for the better pupils to use for practice.

PRACTICE ON ENDINGS, s, ed, ing

The child, in the meantime, is beginning to recognize a few words. As his vocabulary slowly expands, present words to which the common endings of *s, ed,* and *ing* may be added. Let the child practice writing the endings independently many times before adding them to the root words.

Some children will learn to write neatly and accurately within a reasonable time. Other children will learn so slowly that they will require two or three years time to learn to make all of the small letters. They may not even be ready to try to write before they are nine or ten years old.

LENGTH OF WRITING PERIOD

Ten minutes a day is usually enough for an intensive writing practice. It is the persistent daily repetition that results in good writing.

USE OF ALPHABET CHARTS

Alphabet charts should be displayed where the children may easily refer to them. If the children in the group are using both manuscript and cursive forms, these charts should be permanently shown. By looking at the charts when they are undecided about the form of a letter, they may see how to make the correct shape of that letter.

SUMMARY

The teacher should observe the following procedure: Make careful preparation for each writing lesson; set up a definite routine for all directions; assist the children constantly until they gain confidence and are producing legible copy.

7

SPELLING

THE purpose of teaching children to spell is to provide them with a means of communication where oral language cannot be used. The children must be made to realize that there are many everyday events requiring a note or a letter, such as the thank-you note, the letter to a friend or relative, or a note to the teacher.

Motivation for Spelling. Once the child is ready to communicate by writing, he should be allowed to learn to spell some useful words. He may want to give his mother a present and to add his own message. He may ask for help in spelling words or even ask for help in writing the words. That is the time to give him the assistance he wants and to encourage him to complete the message. From such a small beginning, the child may acquire an interest in learning to spell.

Spelling is taught in all areas of school work. The child should be made aware that the words in all of his books, the work on the chalkboard, the worksheets, and workbooks are there to read, to understand, and to use.

Presentation of Essential Words. The words that the child will be using most frequently in writing messages should be taught first in spelling. He should be trained through writing letters or stories to recognize, spell, pronounce, and use them.

Lists of the most frequently used words have been prepared by specialists in this field of study. The teacher should go over several of these lists and prepare one suitable for the children in her room. About one-fourth of the total words used in most oral and written language includes such words as *the, and, is, that, it, to,* and five or six more common words. Therefore, the teacher can see the importance of preparing a short functional list of words and of teaching these words to the children as soon as it is practical.

Presentation of the Alphabet. Before the child can spell, he must know the names of the letters of the alphabet. Authors differ on the order of presentation but agree they should not be taught in alphabetical order, which is learned later.

When the teacher feels that the child has acquired an adequate basic sight vocabulary, she may present the consonant sounds in lessons that are separate from other activities. The sounds should not be presented in isolation, but in combination with a vowel or a word.

The vowels seem best understood when the short sound is presented first. The mentally retarded children remember the sound better if it is presented alone and later put into a word. Games similar to dominoes for matching pictures and vowels, and to Old Maid for matching sets of pictures and words, are useful in arousing interest in learning the short vowel sounds.

The teacher may have the pupils watch the shape of her lips as she makes the sound of the letter, or she may have them look into a mirror and try to imitate the shape of her lips.

As the training in the sounds of the vowels proceeds, the children become aware that the letters *a, e, i, o,* and *u* do not always say the same thing. They learn that the vowel says its name in some words, that it has a short sound in others, and that it takes on yet another sound with some consonants. The different sounds of some of the consonants and the blends which are confusing require much drill and explanation before they are understood.

Children with Speech Difficulties. Good methods of teaching speech should be used for visual and auditory training. In working with the educable mentally retarded, the teacher should be careful that the child is observing her and understands what she is trying to show him. Many mentally retarded children have speech difficulties, which appear to be due to their lack of ability to observe. When they can be induced to look and listen, they begin to imitate and to speak correctly.

Introduction to Formal Spelling. When the child has a sight vocabulary of about fifty words and knows the names and sounds of some of the letters of the alphabet, he is ready for formal spelling. The approach should be through the tactile, as well as through the kinesthetic, auditory, and visual senses.

Stimulation of the Tactile Sense. The tactile sense may be stimulated by *feeling* the shapes of plastic letters, letters cut from felt or cardboard, or letters cut from fine emery paper and glued to cards. The child passes the finger tips over these surfaces, as well as around the outlines of the letters. As the child traces over the letters or words, he repeats the name or sound he is to learn.

Stimulation of the Kinesthetic Sense. The kinesthetic, or muscular sense may be developed by tracing the letters or words on stencils, around plastic letters, over the letters through tracing paper, over the letter forms on the chalkboard, and, with a stick, in the sand box, or in plastic clay that has been smoothed into a shallow pan. The clay, which offers more resistance than the other media, is reserved for helping those with more difficulty in retaining the letter or word forms. As the word is traced in the clay, it is spoken audibly. After this word has been written several times, the clay should be smoothed out and the child should try to write the word or letter from memory. This procedure should be varied with other sense training techniques which are described in this chapter.

Introduction of the Tracing Technique. The teacher should prepare an entire set of the letters of the alphabet and a set of the words the children are learning. The letters or words written on typing or drawing paper with various colored crayons should be several inches tall in either manuscript or cursive. These master sheets should have about eight repetitions to a page, and every other word should be written in a different color crayon. For a suggestion as to the form to use, the teacher should refer to the illustration accompanying this section.

The children use tracing paper over the worksheets, both of which should be arranged where the pupils have easy access to them. As each child traces or copies the words, he must stop at the end of each word and pick up a different colored crayon to resume the copying task. By this act he is made to realize that the word has been completed. He gradually forms a mental picture of the configuration of the word. From this image he begins to see the component parts and finally to realize that the words are composed of individual letters which he must learn to use in order to be able to spell.

Importance of Spelling. Spelling should be taught throughout the school day in connection with every area of learning. The spelling words must be used by the children in oral and written exercises. This continued use will make the words a permanent part of their language.

The teacher should not rely on one series of spelling workbooks for help and inspiration; instead, she should use every resource to provide the educable mentally retarded with adequate spelling materials.

Repetition Needed for Retention. Since these children need much drill on every sound and word, they must have especially prepared worksheets. Only the teacher can provide for the repetition and the practice necessary for the retention of a usable vocabulary. The mastery of even a few simple spelling words is a long and a difficult process. For this reason, the child should have a mental age of about 7-0 years before he is ready to learn to spell. His progress will be very slow. The teacher must not try to hurry him; yet she must keep him moving along. She will find that some children retain the vocabulary very well, while others build up to a plateau and then seem to forget every word. For the latter children there is only one course open, and that is to start over.

SUMMARY

The educable mentally retarded child should acquire a useful written language ability. The spelling words should be selected with care to suit his present and his adult requirements. The words should be presented to him in a slow but continuous process to assure their retention.

8

MUSIC

THE purpose of teaching music to the educable mentally retarded is to assist them to a greater enjoyment of music.

Basis for Planning a Music Program. The teacher, in planning a music course for mentally retarded children, must consider their mental, physical and emotional status, as well as their environmental background. She must have a knowledge of their char-

26. Rhythm Band.

acteristics, abilities, and disabilities. She must know their peculiar problems of learning, discipline, humor, social situations, and group activities in order to have success with them. She must have an understanding of their mental, physical, and emotional needs as opposed to the normal child's needs.

She must learn how to hold their interest, to present adequate materials, and to assist in comprehension. She must learn ways to care for the maladjusted or the physically handicapped in the class. She must learn to recognize when a child has reached the saturation point with a certain type of music and change to another activity. Some of these special techniques are explained and listed in this chapter.

There may be in the group a child who has not been diagnosed as brain damaged, but who responds to loud music and a fast tempo with shrieks of laughter or tears. He may require special care, even to being removed from the group before such an activity is started, because he has a low tolerance for this type of sound.

The teacher must remember that the educable mentally retarded child has a short attention span; therefore, she should vary the instruction period with several types of activity, commensurate with the child's ability.

Special Training Is Necessary for the Teacher. The teacher, friends, and relatives of the educable mentally retarded often forget in their planning or their expectations that these children are sub-normal mentally and that, as such, possess certain inherent disabilities that no amount of training can overcome. The physically handicapped person cannot grow a new hand or leg that has been severed or damaged, but he can learn to get along very well with the use of artificial limbs. However, there is no such hope for the child who possesses a deficient or a damaged brain. True, he can learn to use the undamaged portion of the brain with the help of well-trained teachers and understanding parents, but he cannot substitute anything for the part of the brain that is not functioning.

The untrained person, through his blundering, hinders the child's progress by disturbing him emotionally. Conversely, the trained person will do everything possible to create successful situations by eliminating feelings of frustration and failure. The music period should be a happy experience for these children. The teacher must love both music and the retarded children to be successful. These children are very perceptive of false sentiments and quickly detect anyone who assumes superiority or who makes them an object of ridicule.

Types of Activities. These activities may be rearranged as the children's moods and needs arise. While an outline for the entire year may be made, it should be flexible enough to utilize items related to the units being taught. It should also be enjoyable, as well as instructional. The following activities are suitable for the educable mentally retarded:

1. New and old songs for the fun of singing.
2. Standard songs that everyone should know—"The Star Spangled Banner;" "America:" song of one's own state; seasonal songs.
3. Recordings of musical scores of famous works, such as "The Nutcracker" and "Peter and the Wolf."
4. Films or film-strips to accompany the musical works.
5. Understanding of various musical instruments.
6. Playing some instrument—bells, xylophone, drum.
7. Playing rhythm instruments.
8. Singing to recordings.
9. Drawing to music.
10. Taking physical exercise to music.
11. Learning songs by rote.
12. Playing musical games.
13. Learning square and modern dancing.
14. Learning folk dances of other countries.

Teaching Songs with the Words and Music. The teacher should observe the following order:

1. Write the words of the song on the chalkboard or chart paper.
2. Use the words of the song as a reading lesson, explaining the meaning of the words and phrases.
3. Present the tune by humming or playing on a musical instrument.

4. Have the children hum the tune.
5. Sing the words to the children.
6. Repeat this procedure during several lessons.

A FOLK DANCE

The Tinikling Dance. The Tinikling Dance was introduced to a group of intermediate age educable mentally retarded children by a graduate student teacher from the Philippine Islands. This dance provided the focus of interest for a unit of work about the growing of rice. The teacher used the music and words in both Spanish and English. The Tinikling is a Samar-Leyte folksong with the English version by Nancy Byrd Turner. The name of the song and dance, **Tinikling,** differs in its spelling from the name of the bird, **tikling.** The teacher demonstrated and explained how the tikling runs and hops around as it pecks at the rice and tries to keep out of the trap which is represented by two poles.

27. The Tinikling—a folk dance.

The directions and explanation of the meaning of the dance are simple as given in the music text, *The Philippine Progressive Music Series*, Primary Grades, Copyright, 1948, by Silver Burdett Company, in the Republic of the Philippines. "The name 'Tinikling' suggests the imitation of the way in which the bird 'tikling' walks. Use the right foot for four measures, then the left for four and keep alternating."

The dance is easy to learn. The three-quarter time provides an easy rhythm for the dancers as they hop on one foot as the poles are brought together, and tap that foot inside the "trap" as the poles are separated on the counts of *two* and *three*.

The teacher and the children may make up a story about the tikling bird and the trap and act it out to the music of the song. The children enjoy an activity such as this one in which they learn something that their brothers and sisters have not learned at school. Every community has some members from other nations who are usually delighted to teach folk songs and dances. Perhaps some of the children's parents or relatives might be willing to help in such a project.

The teacher can locate many recordings and books of instruction to help her in presenting similar material from our own country. Some square dances are simple, and the children enjoy the rhythms and the activities. Colorful scarves and skirts help to secure interest in the folk dances.

SUMMARY

The educable mentally retarded enjoy music. With a patient teacher they can learn many songs, rhythms, musical games, and dances. In these activities she can also help improve their ability to socialize.

9

ART

PURPOSE OF THE ART PROGRAM

THE purpose of teaching art to the educable mentally retarded is to give them an opportunity to learn about some of the materials used in art work. It should also help to lessen their fears, tensions, and pressures, as well as provide recreation.

Planning the Art Program for the Educable Mentally Retarded. Art activities should be planned so that the mentally retarded are able to achieve success and attain a degree of pleasure. Therefore, the program must be adapted to the children's ability to understand and to follow directions. The teacher must remember that a simple direction may contain words that have no meaning for the children. Their useful vocabulary is limited because of a dearth of experiences.

Mentally retarded children usually have a feeling of frustration whenever they are introduced to any of the tools used in creative endeavor. Their undertakings have been unsatisfactory compared to those of their chronologically aged peers. Any plan or directions should be carefully prepared by the teacher so that the directions and the skills needed to complete the task do not frustrate the child before he even attempts it.

Basis for Planning the Program. The teacher must consider the chronological age of the children, as well as their emotional tone in the preparation of an art lesson. A child cannot respond to this instruction when he is terrified, insecure because of parental rejection, or is angry at misunderstood or cruel treatment. Such children are unable to verbalize their feelings or to interpret to themselves the treatment they have received at home, at school, or at play; hence a free period of art activity should be substituted for the regular class lesson.

The teacher must be aware that in every educable mentally retarded class there are at least three groups with as many years of experience in that room. Since each pupil remains there approximately three years, about one-third of them are new to the program, one-third have had one year's experience, and the other third have two year's experience.

The teacher should carefully list the skills needed to complete the project before deciding whether all of the group can complete it or whether this is a project for a few of the older children. The mentally retarded do not notice how things are done around the home; they do not have a supply of miscellaneous information that helps them in carrying out directions; their environment usually does not provide them with experiences in cutting, sewing, ironing, stirring things with spoons, or rolling out pie dough. Any such skill must be taught by the teacher before the child is ready to proceed with directions calling for cutting, pressing, mixing, rolling out or sewing.

The teacher inexperienced in working with the mentally retarded is often misled by the appearance of these children, for physically they differ little from the normal children. Therein lies the danger for the children and for the teacher. Since they do not appear to be handicapped, she expects them to perform as does the usual child, but they are unable to meet even the ordinary competition of their peers.

The mentally retarded lose their self-esteem because of their many failures to meet with approval and success; as a result, they sink into apathy or indulge in tantrums, bullying, or other overt actions. However, success in even a small measure contributes to building their ego by compensating for failure in many endeavors.

The educable mentally retarded have little true imagination or creative ability. Fortunately, many of them, blessed with imitative ability, are able to enlarge upon this with delightful fantasy. They love gay colors, and when they feel free to do as they desire with a medium, obtain much joy and pleasure from their efforts.

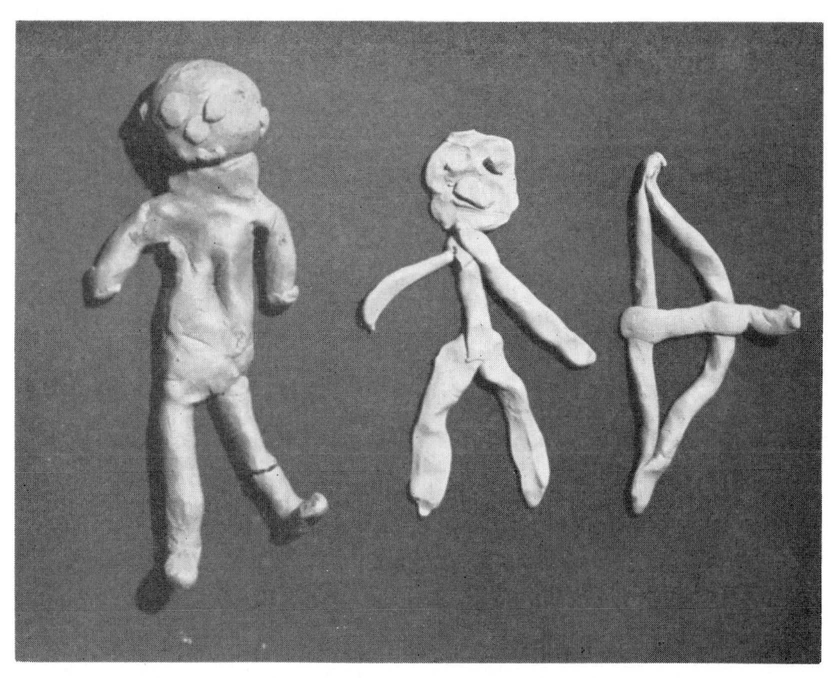

28. The clay images show a lack of self-confidence.

Developing Self-confidence. The teacher will observe that once the child feels unrestricted and free to paint, the urge to do so occurs frequently. Some children have repressed their feelings so long that it takes much time, patience, understanding, and encouragement to get them to realize that the teacher wants them to be unrestrained.

Children who have been in regular rooms find it difficult to abandon the previous teacher's standards of perfection. It is only after they accept the new evaluation and relax that they can tell their story through their own fantasy of painting or modeling in clay.

For many months Joe was rebellious toward every school activity, his modeling in clay was flat, immature, and repetitious. Gradually, his appearance became that of a happy youth, his progress in the basic school subjects improved, his modeling became three dimensional, varied and coordinated with units of study.

29. The clay images show developing self-confidence.

The teacher can help the emotionally disturbed child by giving him materials and a place to work in privacy. He then may gain confidence not only in himself, but in the teacher. This confidence cannot be forced, but must grow slowly as rapport is established.

The child's confidence in the teacher may cause him to take a painting to her and even try to tell her a little story about it. If possible, she may write down the story and later use it as a reading lesson with the child. If it is not a suitable story, she may want to pin it to the picture or model for future reference. These acts on the teacher's part usually give the child a sense of importance which makes the painting and story valuable to him. Such rapport between pupils and teacher may take weeks or months to be established.

Such was the case of Gladys who was a product of a broken home and of several unsatisfactory foster home placements. Gladys was a pale, withdrawn child who refused to speak except in monosyllables. She was five years educationally retarded and was not interested in any school activity. She would sit at a table

30. At the time the clay images were made, the child was withdrawn and spoke only in monosyllables.

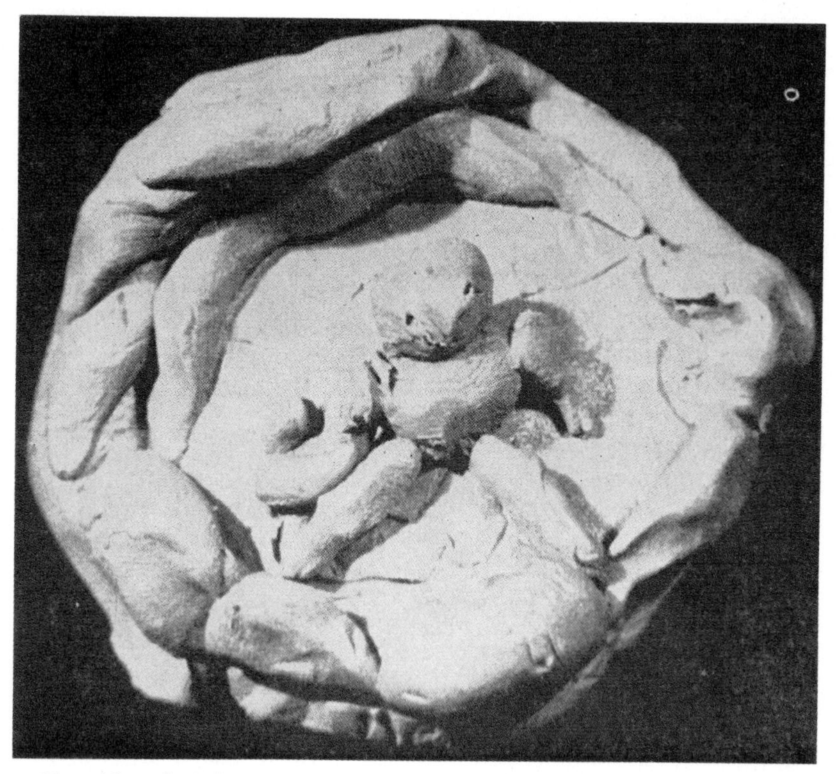

31. After this clay image was made, the child spoke her first sentence.

32. Allan modeled comic faces.

with a ball of clay and withdraw from the activity of the classroom. She made a few objects but quickly destroyed them.

It was the middle of February before she brought one of her modelings to the teacher. She called it "Little Mouse." Later she made some objects she identified as "Little Boy and Kitty," and "Cat and Kitten." It was almost a month before she saved another object. She worked for about an hour rolling, patting, destroying, and again shaping the object. She brought this to the teacher and said, "This is Little Boy sitting in his bed."

This was the first long statement she had made and the teacher was elated. After that Gladys began to take part in class discussions and other activities.

In working with the children on a free basis, the teacher instructs them to put their names and the date on the back of the paper. A mark of their name or initials on the clay will establish ownership. The mentally retarded frequently refuse to acknowledge as their own production a painting in as short a time as a few hours. The child cannot recall the emotion that produced the painting. Since he has painted it out of his system, he does not feel kinship with the painting.

Allan never claimed any of his clay models. However, his modeling seemed to help him relax sufficiently to participate in class discussion as well as make progress in the basic skills of reading, writing, and arithmetic.

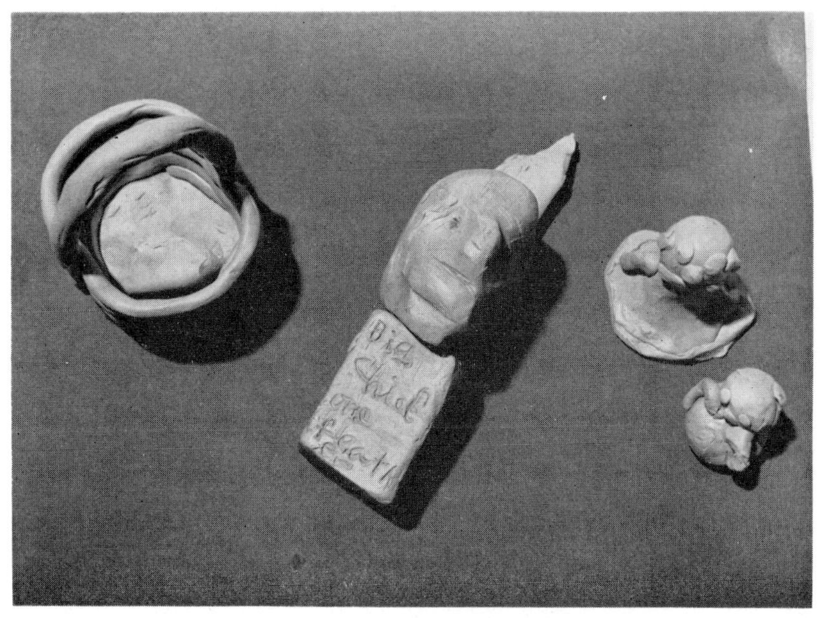

33. Allan modeled three-dimensional figures.

The painting of a picture or the modeling of an object appears to be the releasing of sub-conscious drives. Sometimes the child appears lost to his surroundings as he works, whether he is at the easel using the large brushes with poster paint or at his desk with crayons or at a table with finger paint or clay. At such a time no one should approach him to speak about or to direct his activity. The release of tension is the important thing at this particular time. For this child as with everyone else, the joy is in the making of the object. Any interruption of his absorption in his activity blocks the release of tension.

Instructing the Pupils. The child will get more satisfaction and emotional relief from a misshapen little bowl that he did alone than from a beautiful product largely shaped by the teacher's guiding hand. Teachers often both consciously and unconsciously structure the children's work.

The teacher does the child a disfavor when she smooths out the clay dog, suggests the color it should be painted, and even paints it for him. She is not helping his mental health when she adds a knowing line to a drawing or reshapes a face or form. The child immediately knows that his product has been rejected. It is no longer his very own. He must be allowed to complete the project in his own way from the first brushful of paint or lump of clay to the finished product.

Because of their inability to sustain interest over a long period of time, any project that is planned for the educable mentally retarded should be one that can be completed within two or three lessons. The teacher must also remember that, since these children have a very short attenion span, lessons should not extend over thirty minutes. Frustrated by an activity that continues over a prolonged period of time, they often show their resentment by tantrums, sulking, spoiling materials, or being absent on art days.

Lessons of instruction on how to use the different art materials should be just a trial period with plenty of time for informal questions and answers. The teacher must remember, when giving the directions, that each detail must be explained, for these children

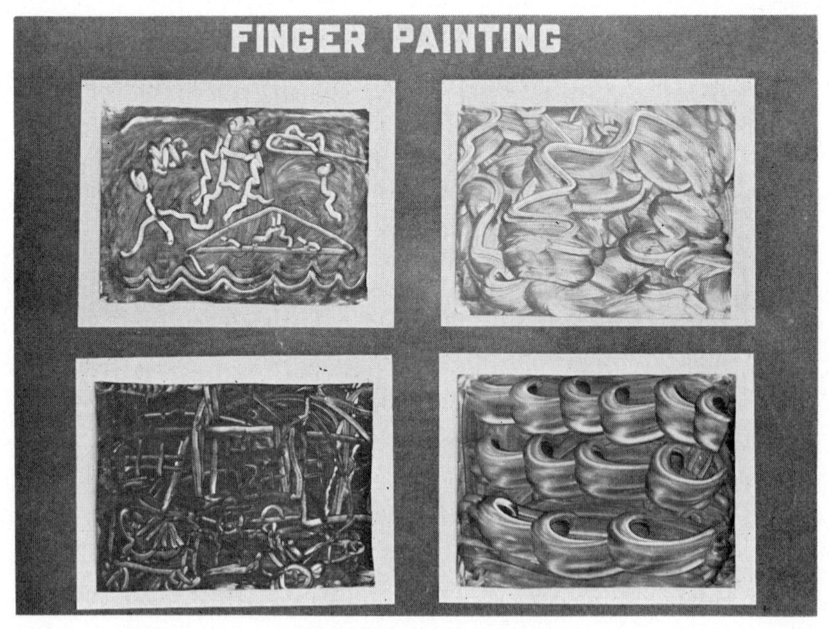

34. Finger Painting.

35. The girls are weaving place mats.

frequently do not understand but hesitate to ask for explanations, even saying they understand when they do not.

The directions should be given orally, as few of the written words used would be in the children's sight vocabulary. Any direction on the chalkboard must be in clear round letters with well-separated words which must be explained. These words must be taught as patiently as in any reading lesson. For many of the younger children in the group even these simple directions will usually be incomprehensible.

The Classroom Teacher and the Special Art Teacher. If the classroom teacher is directing the art and crafts class, she can control the presentation of the work to the children. Since she is in constant contact with the pupils, she knows their abilities and potentialities. However, if there is an art teacher who comes in once or twice a week, it is usually better to attempt no coordination between classwork and the art program. The homeroom

36. Crafts produced by educable mentally retarded children in the classroom. Children's chronological ages were from 10 to 13 years.

teacher must find time in her schedule to do the art and craft work that she feels is required to complete a unit of study.

Finger Painting. The inarticulate child, who is unable to express his emotion, finds a medium in finger painting that he can easily use. Because he can freely express his likes and dislikes with color and muscular action, he obtains great emotional relief and also a feeling of accomplishment through the manipulation of the paint.

When a child fully accepts finger painting, it is a satisfying and meaningful experience. There is the emotional impact of the chosen color mingled with the tactual and kinesthetic process. The child is unconsciously dramatizing his past in the swirls and lines of the slightly resistant medium of the paint.

The table that the teacher provides for the finger painting should be near a sink or a large pan of water. A pad of several

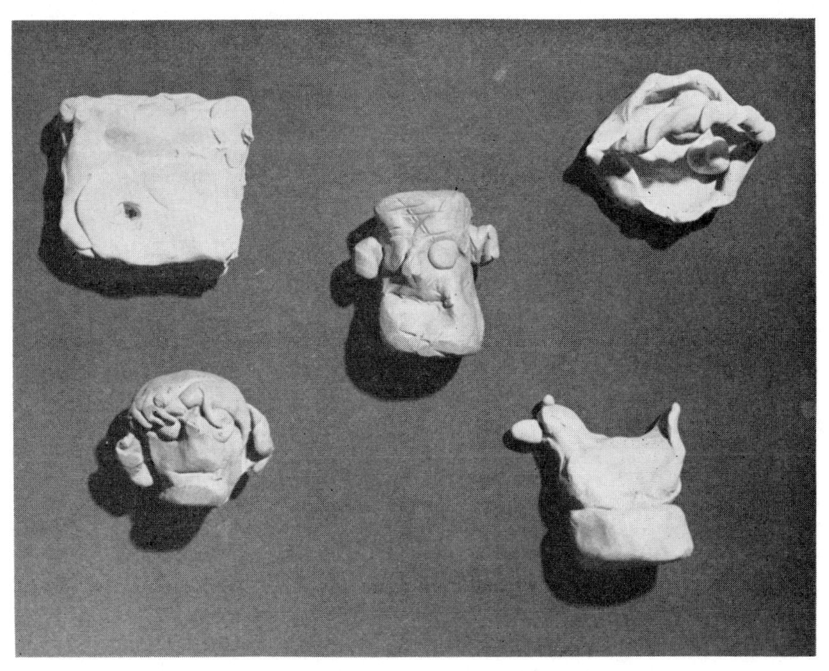

37. Tim copied faces and objects from the movies.

newspapers may be placed at one end of the table to protect it from the paint. The paper for finger painting, which may be the regular kind or white wrapping paper, is dipped into water and placed, slick side up, on the pile of newspapers. The paint may be purchased in jars or made like starch and colored with powder paint. A large spoonful of the paint is placed on the wet paper, after which the child spreads the paint around with his hands. He forms such patterns and pictures as his fancy dictates.

Varied Results Produced by the Free Art Experiences. The educable mentally retarded will become absorbed in making pictures that repeat the same design over and over for many months with few variations. This design is a reflection of the child's personality and peculiar problem.

A change in environment may effect a change in a child's painting. He may be so sensitive to his surroundings that he quickly expresses his feelings in some form. If an art medium is

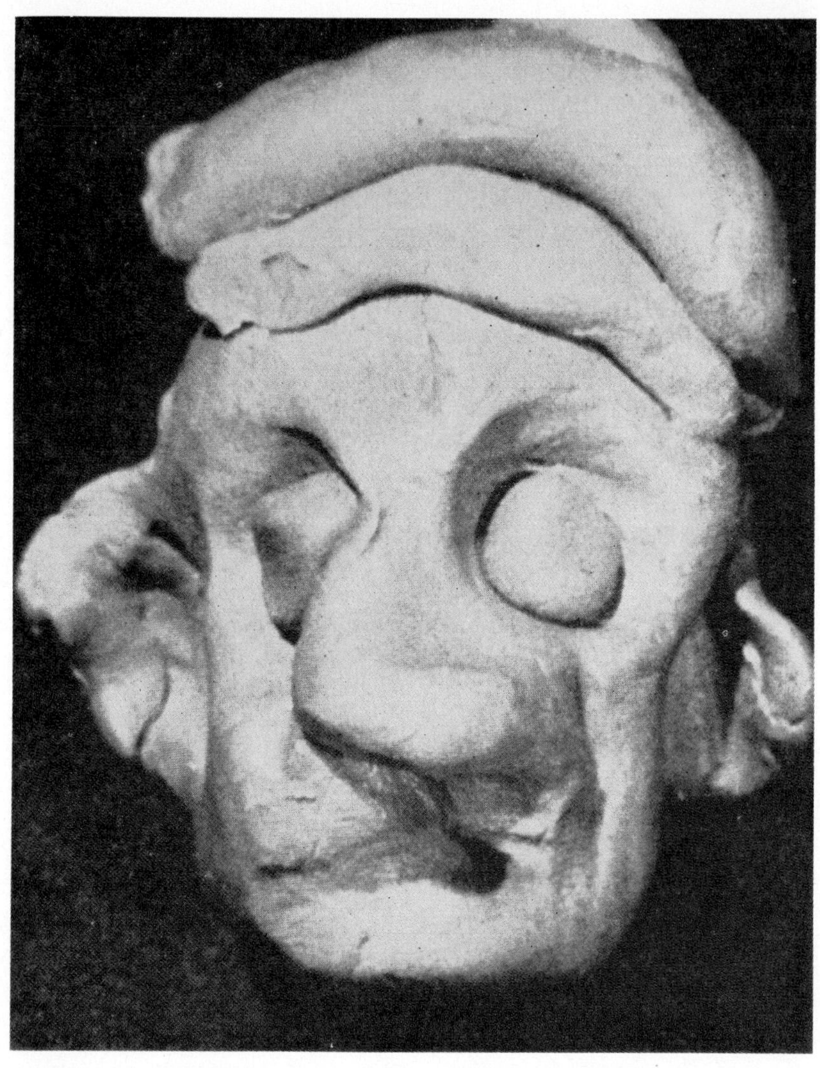

38. Tim copied faces from comic books.

39. Crayon Drawings.

convenient, he will use that form to express his insecurity, tension, hostility, happiness, or love.

Types of Art and Crafts for the Educable Mentally Retarded. The educable mentally retarded like to work with things that seem useful. They also like to make pretty things. They are intrigued with such simple crafts as stick painting, making puppets from socks or paper sacks, knitting on frames, tooling leather or copper, or enameling on copper. They enjoy daubing water colors or poster paint on paper. After they have made a small ball of clay into a bird or a rabbit, they can glaze it and place it in the kiln. They enjoy watching it being transformed into a shining object in the color of their choice.

Some educable mentally retarded children have an ability for copying drawings or pictures in detail. However, the child who deviates from the pattern and shows originality may be a child who is not functioning as high as his true ability. Tim was a child who loved to copy faces he had seen in comic books or in the movies. He used clay as his medium for expression. He did not attempt to do original characters. This form of modeling does not appear to result in much emotional release, but the pounding and shaping of the clay does seem to release muscular tension.

The mentally retarded enjoy using crayons. Many will illustrate their stories by imitating the drawings or pictures from books. Dependent upon a copy, they are seldom able to adapt a picture to a new purpose. They find it difficult to do freehand paper cutting, because they lack the imagination to visualize an object in its true proportions when greatly reduced in size. They need to view a completed pattern from which to work.

SUMMARY

The educable mentally retarded will benefit from an art program that is administered with patience and understanding. The mentally retarded cannot be forced to accomplish things for which they have little ability and in which they have no interest.

The program that is best for the mentally retarded is one that does not restrict nor coerce, yet engenders enthusiasm. By careful direction, it increases skill in the manipulation of the art and crafts materials.

10

AUDIO-VISUAL AND OTHER SENSORY TRAINING

PURPOSE OF USING AUDIO-VISUAL AND SENSORY MATERIALS

THE mentally retarded child will learn more readily from audio-visual and sensory materials than he will from lectures or explanations.

Kinds of Materials. Too often one thinks of sound films as being synonymous with audio-visual materials. However, other audio-visual materials assist in stimulating the interest, add to the field of information, and aid in retention.

There are many avenues to explore in this field. Among these are films, film-strips, slides, photographs, paintings, magazines and books, charts, maps, dioramas, peep boxes, radio, television, phonograph records, field trips, materials brought into the classroom, dramatizations, puppet plays, shadow plays and games. The list is almost limitless.

SELECTION OF AUDIO-VISUAL MATERIALS

When selecting material to bring new experiences to children, the teacher should have in mind some of the basic values and aims in using the audio-visual materials. She should also consider the maturity and the abilities of the children who use them. The group must be ready for the material when it is presented. If it is on an interest level comparable with their chronological age, they will feel it is worthy of their attention. The materials, which

40. Visual material.

must be simple, should recognize the dominant interest pertaining to the topic being studied.

Films. Films are the most frequently used of all audio-visual materials. They are prepared to teach certain facts, to assist in the understanding of definite skills, and to develop desirable attitudes. Sound films are available in color, as well as in black and white. The usual educational film for children runs for about eleven minutes. A short length film is better than a long one to retain the attention and interest of the educable mentally retarded.

Most school systems have their own film library or belong to a district or county exchange through which films, film-strips, and recordings may be requisitioned. The teachers are usually provided with lists of such materials.

Many films are also available for the cost of transportation. Some companies charge only for the return postage. The advertising in such films is usually inconspicuous and not at all objectionable.

If the school board does not furnish the needed records, films, and materials for the class, usually some civic group will help out with funds for renting and transporting them.

The film should be secured far enough ahead of the showing to pre-view it. Class preparation for the film may consist of the following steps: Explain why the film is being shown; ask the children to watch for particular things in the film in order to be prepared to discuss them after returning to the classroom.

It is a good plan to scatter the children about the room and if possible to have a vacant seat between each one. Best friends sitting side by side to view a film too often want to talk instead of look at the film.

After the children see the film, there should be a discussion period, during which a list of their comments is written on the chalkboard. Their thinking should be directed to bring out items that require emphasis for the subject under study and to correlate the new information with previous lessons. If possible, the film should be shown later to clear up misunderstandings or to emphasize certain points.

Effective Field Trips. To be effective, field trips need not be taken to far away places. Every community has many interesting and helpful places available for school tours. A trip to a local store, post office, fire station, bakery, a near-by farm, museum, or library may be rewarding. The trip and the experience should meet the child's need.

The teacher should make careful preparation for a trip of this kind, whether it is for one hour to a local store or all day to a large museum. She should make plans far enough ahead to avoid confusion among either the children or their parents.

If the children are to leave the school grounds, parental permission should be obtained. The teacher should discuss carefully with the group the following procedure: the purpose of the trip; things they will see; possible questions they should ask; the kind of clothes they should wear; the kind of lunch to take; the place where the lunch will be eaten; the opportunities for getting a drink and for toileting; the time of departure and return; the amount of spending money allowed; courtesy; manners; and safety.

The teacher must insist that the group stay together so that there will be no rushing ahead to be first in line. Everyone should wait for the teacher to direct them in crossing streets, entering buildings, and viewing exhibits. After the field trip each child should be given an opportunity to relate his experiences. With the help of the teacher the children will write these stories to be used later in reading and review lessons. Words are selected from the stories for spelling and for writing lessons.

Some of the children will want to write their own stories. They may need some help with spelling. They will enjoy reading their own stories to the class.

Every child should have an opportunity to illustrate his story. Individual drawings may be put on the bulletin board. These usually depict a variety of scenes with whimsical forms and gay use of color.

Training of the Senses. Mentally retarded children need special training of the senses. They will look off into the distance when the teacher is presenting a lesson on a chart or is writing on the board. Their listlessness and lack of attention are shown by their unwillingness to use a marker under a line of words. The teacher should insist upon its use, because it does focus their attention on the words.

These children must be taught to use their senses to help them retain an impression of the world in which they live. Games may be devised for training the visual, auditory, tactile, kinesthetic, taste, and olfactory senses to recognize things with which they come in contact.

The mentally retarded should be made aware of the meaning of these terms: hot, cold, warm, cool, sour, sweet, bitter, salt, pungent odors, high and low tones, smooth and rough surfaces, far and near, similar and different, colors and sounds.

ACTIVITIES FOR TRAINING THE SENSES

1. Place some different articles in a box. They may be a plastic toy car, a red ribbon, a paper clip, and an eraser. Show the articles to the child for a minute and ask him what he saw. He may be able to name just one thing. Try again. Repeat this for several times each day until he is able to name all of the articles.

   If the child is very slow, use only two or three articles at first. Then increase the number of articles until he is able to name four or five things from a one minute glance. Change the contents of the box and continue this as long as it is effective.

2. Show the child different kinds of scraps of cloth. Allow him to handle them and become familiar with the names of such materials as cotton, linen, wool, velvet, and silk. This may take days or weeks before the names of the materials are established.

   Play a game using the cloth scraps. Place them in a bag and allow the child to feel the materials and select one at a time. Let him name the material before taking it from the bag. If he identifies it correctly, let him take a colored counter from a box for a tally. If he fails to give the correct name, tell him the name and put the material back in the bag. He can count the tallies and keep a record. If he is unable to write the number, the teacher may do it for him. This will provide motivation to learn to count and to make the numbers.

3. Cut construction paper of different colors into squares, triangles, circles, and oblongs. Paste small strips of felt or fuzzy paper to the backs of the strips. The child may then use the flannel board to group the shapes according to color, size, or form.

4. Games of lotto are excellent for matching. The teacher may buy commercial games, or she may, with the help of the pupils, prepare sets. The backs of tablets, suit boxes, or tagboard are good to use for the base of the game. Cut pictures or words from magazines in the category needed and paste

them in orderly rows in squares on the cardboard. Paste the matching pictures or words on small squares to be used by the children to mark their recognition of a word or picture. Build similar games for teaching units about foods, transportation, clothing, health, safety, animals, plants, the letters of the alphabet, and new words.

5. Make scrapbooks of pictures illustrating beginning sounds of words. Concentrate on one sound at a time. The preferable letter is the one being taught in writing or in phonics. The child should write the letter at the top of the page in the scrap book. Help him to find in an old magazine a picture that shows the beginning sound correctly. Let him paste the picture on the page under the letter of the alphabet. If you think he knows what to do or if he wants to work alone, let him try.

   When the child has found a picture that he thinks belongs to the page, tell him to bring it to you to be checked *before* he pastes it in the scrap book. Have him say the word aloud before the picture is pasted in the books so that he experiences hearing the sound and associates it with the beginning letter of the word.

   Have the child write the beginning letter under the picture, followed by a line to indicate there are more letters in the word, such as b—— under a picture of a ball.

6. Let the children construct a domino game of matching colors which involves drill with the use of the ruler and skill in using the pencil and crayons. Use lightweight cardboard for the dominoes. Draw across the cardboard lines forming rectangles 1½ x 3 inches. Cut the domino shapes apart, leaving two rectangles fastened end to end.

   The children should color the dominoes with crayons. They may assign colors to the numbers from 0 to 5, as 0—black; 1—blue; 2—green; 3—yellow; 4—brown; 5—red. Lay out a set of real dominoes and help the children to see how many of each color are needed.

   Play the game by matching the colors. Each child should name aloud the color he is matching. As soon as the names of the colors are learned, change to cards of different colors. For example, take out all of the green ones and add purple. Continue until the children recognize all of the colors.

7. Make another kind of matching game from old cloth swatch, or sample, cards, that may be secured from stores. Cut the cards into two pieces to be used for matching color, texture, and pattern.
8. Make cards to teach the opposites or comparisons. Use pictures from magazines or draw the illustrations for such words as big—little; more—less; black—white; rough—smooth. Show one card and let the child find the opposite.

   Arrange the cards on two tables and let the child match them. Later clip the words to the cards. After the child gains confidence in matching the pictures and words, remove the pictures and match the words. Words meaning opposites and comparisons are difficult for the mentally retarded to remember and comprehend.
9. Take the children for a walk around the block, for the purpose of enabling each one to draw a picture of something he has seen. This can be a seasonal activity, such as new leaves, the snow, or the birds' nests. The children's ability to observe, to tell what they saw, and to depict in drawings these things will improve after a few such walks.
10. Play games on the chalkboard to show likenesses and differences. Draw circles, squares, ovals, oblongs, or triangles. Put lines or decorations on them in colored chalk to incite interest and to help the children observe more closely. The children choose teams to play a relay game. The teacher may appoint captains to keep the scores. Each member of the team has one chance to show the change that was made by the teacher on the drawing. The one who is **It** marks a tally on the board if he recognizes the change in the detail of the drawing, a zero if he does not identify it.
11. Make a game of watching for shapes in the clouds. Draw the shapes on blue paper with white chalk.
12. Give each child a leaf that has been picked from a tree or shrub on the playground. Match the leaf with another one

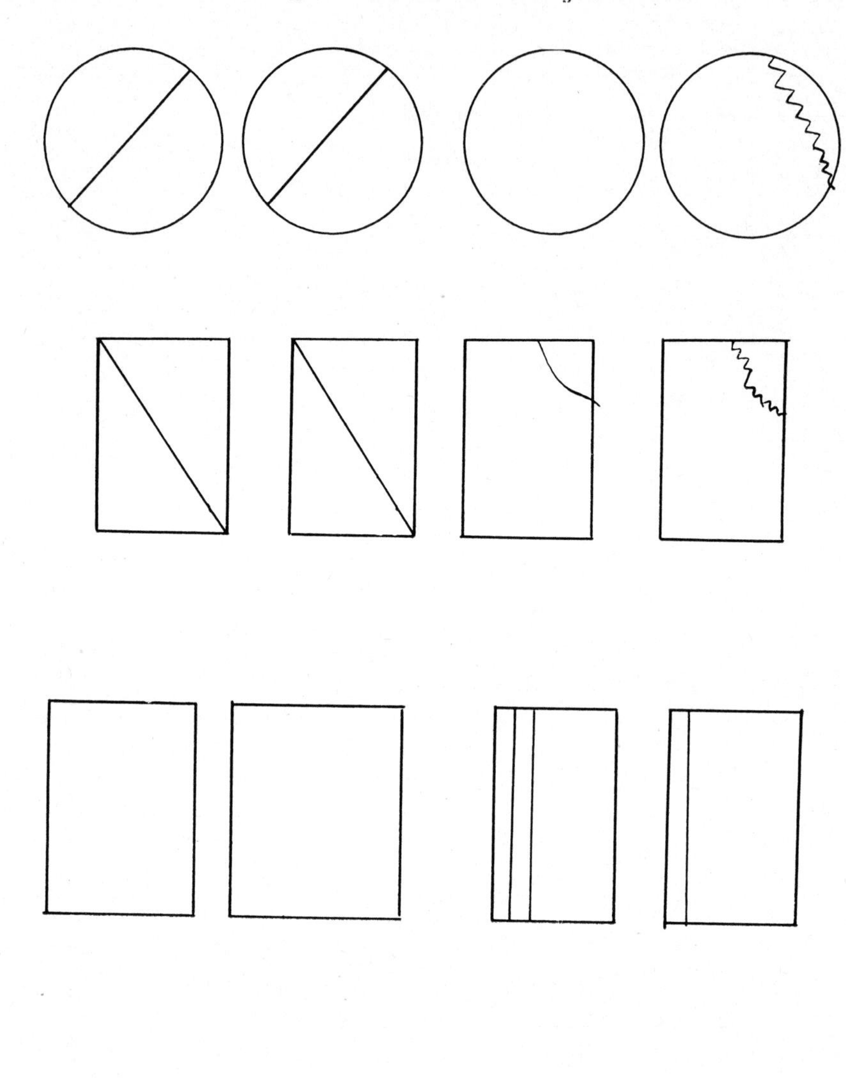

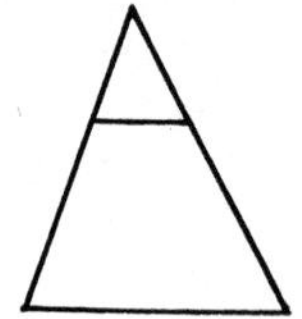

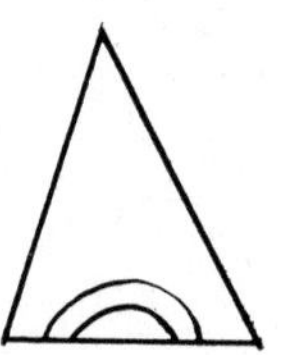

41. Examples of designs for finding differences and likenesses.

from the playground. Learn to identify the trees and the shrubs by their leaves.

13. Train the hearing by learning to listen to voices, to the soft music of a phonograph, to the rhythm of singing voices, to people walking, to the wind in a tree, to the buzz of a bee or a fly, to the bounce of a ball, or to a bell being struck softly.
14. Teach the child to listen for directions and to pay attention while a direction is being completed; to listen to a message so that he will be able to deliver it promptly and correctly; or to read or to listen to a story for better comprehension and retention.

SUMMARY

The teacher must use every lesson and activity to train the eyes and the ears, which must do extra duty for the educable mentally retarded.

11

THE BULLETIN BOARD

MATERIALS AND THEIR USE

Selection of Materials Is Important. The teacher should carefully select the materials to be placed on the bulletin board, since it plays an important part in the teaching of mentally retarded children. It should be attractive with color, variety, and simple materials which stand out and invite attention. A large number of pictures and materials on display cause the children to ignore everything on the board. Materials should be changed frequently and brought back later if the teacher needs them for review.

Arrangement of Materials Is Important. The bulletin board may be neatly divided into sections by using heavy cord or plastic tape. Each section should have a title or subtitle, and the children should be briefed on the meaning of every word used.

Lettering and Titles Are Important. The titles should be in bold, eye-catching letters cut on simple lines. One color of paper is best for the letters of the titles, since a word cut from two or more colors is confusing to the vision. The word *Washington* cut with letters of red, white, and blue might not be recognizable as one word by the educable mentally retarded. The letters may be shadow cut by using one contrasting color under another or made more prominent by the use of a contrasting color for mounting purposes.

Pictures Should Be Large. Pictures that are used on the bulletin board should be only those that can be plainly seen from any part of the school room. If a picture with much detail must be used, the teacher should be sure the children have an opportunity to

42. Lettering and titles are important.

43. Children's construction work should be displayed.

look at it closely. Sometimes she should prepare a section of the bulletin board for humorous pictures just for fun for the children. Humorous animal pictures generally win a good response from the pupils. The teacher must remember that the humor of the mentally retarded is not subtle but is very practical and even rowdy.

Displays Should Be Changed Frequently. One section of the bulletin board may be reserved for material concerned with the current unit of study. The topic of the unit should be in a conspicuous place. The charts, maps, poster pictures, and exhibits should be changed from day to day as new material is introduced in the unit.

Displays Should Be Mounted. The displays should all be mounted to form an attractive picture. Small items may be grouped on a large card to form a pleasing arrangement. Then the teacher should walk about the room and view it from various places to judge its appeal and decide if there could be a more harmonious or effective placement.

Children's Contributions Are Important. A space should be provided for the children's contributions. The teacher may place a large sheet of construction paper on the bulletin board and stick a few pins near it for attaching materials to the board. The children themselves put up the interesting items they bring and talk about their items during a sharing period.

Pupils' paintings, drawings, booklets, murals, and construction work in art and crafts should be displayed. Such material may be kept for only a day or two, but the pupils gain much satisfaction from seeing it exhibited.

SUPPLEMENTARY MATERIALS TO THE BULLETIN BOARD

A table may be used as a supplement to the bulletin board for presenting materials used in connection with the unit being studied, such as reference books, or equipment. There should be other places about the room for such activities as cutting and pasting, clay modeling, painting, reading, science projects, storage for records and music, and a phonograph.

SUMMARY

Properly used, the bulletin board with accessory displays assists in focusing the children's attention on the materials they are studying.

12

THE SOCIOGRAM

THE PURPOSE OF THE SOCIOGRAM

THE teacher of the educable mentally retarded will find a simple sociogram helpful in discovering areas of friction and confusion that are disrupting the personal relationships among members of the class.

PROCEDURE

The teacher who is unfamiliar with the procedure of giving and evaluating a sociogram should study a text on the subject in order to secure the maximum benefit from the results of one. She can obtain adequate information, however, by preparing simple questions to ask each member of the group. These may be affirmative or negative questions or a combination of the two which may concern the relationships between pupils and their activities at school, at play, and at home.

The questions should not be presented to the entire group but be asked individually. There is a tendency by the pupils to look around the group and to make signals to each other or to ask questions, thereby revealing their choices which influence the answers of others. The teacher will find that this attempt will be made even though the questions are administered individually but with less influence on the results.

The teacher must maintain an objective and detached attitude toward the replies and attempt to encourage each child to answer each question, yet not to pressure him nor influence his reply.

A form for the sociogram may be similar to the following list of affirmative and negative questions.

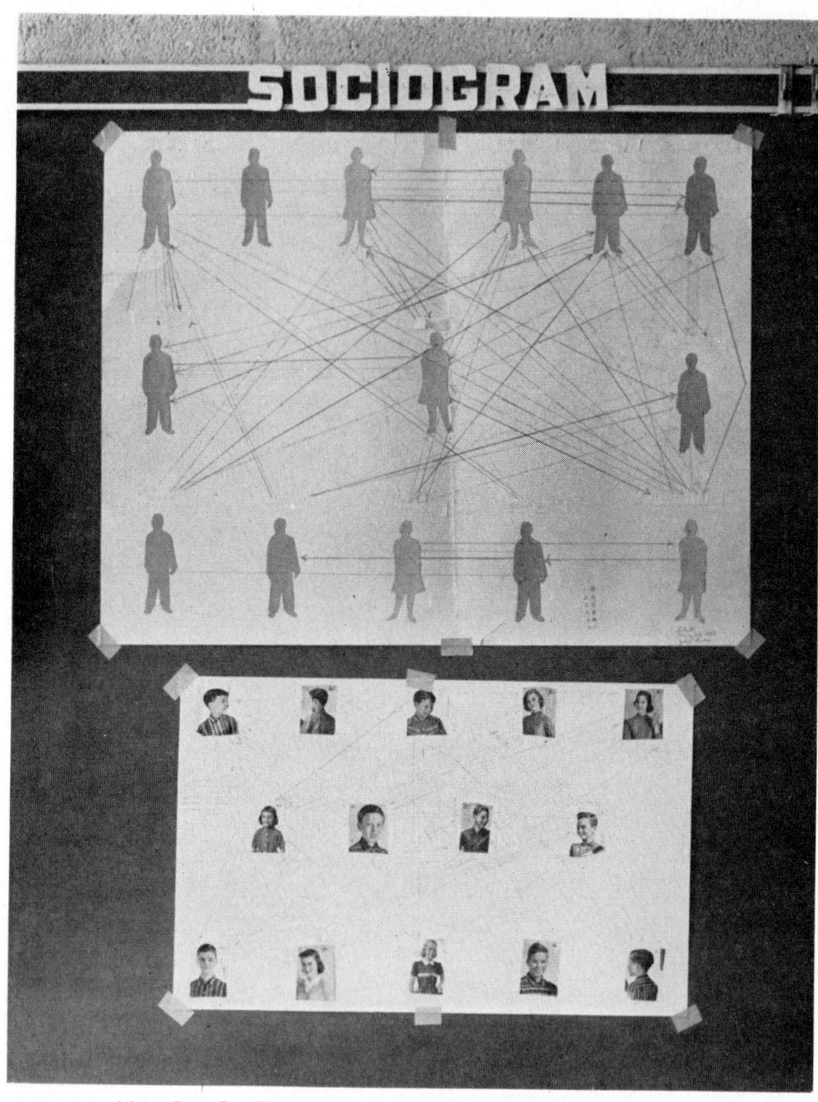

44. Graphs illustrating complete results of a sociogram.

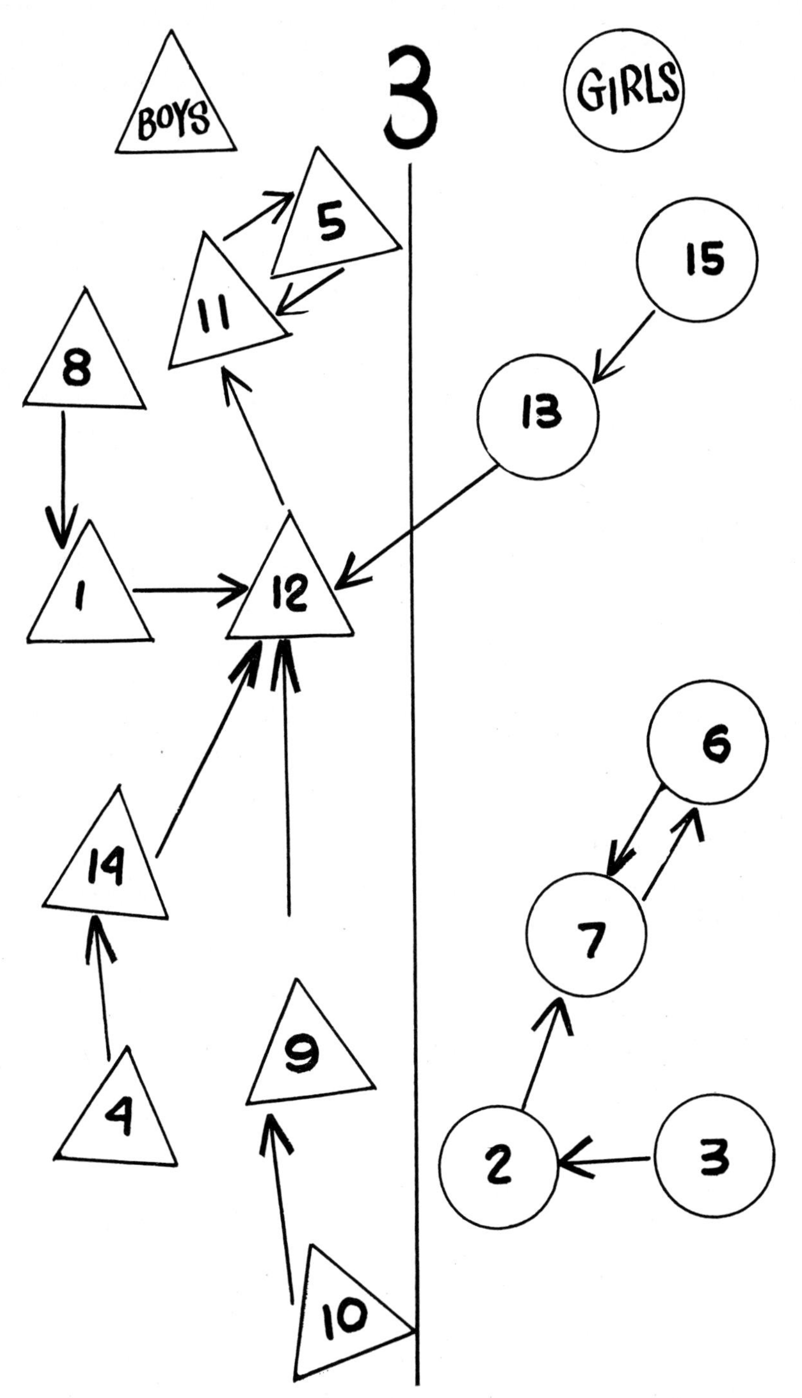

45. Graph illustrating results from one question on a sociogram.

QUESTIONS FOR A SOCIOGRAM

1. Whom would you like to sit by in school?
2. Whom would you rather not sit by in school?
3. Whom would you like for a partner in a game?
4. Whom would you rather not have for a partner in a game?
5. Whose home would you like to visit?
6. Whom would you rather not have to visit you in your home?

The above set of questions concerns three different situations; the schoolroom; the playtime; the home. It is sometimes a shock to the teacher to discover a pupil who has been neither accepted nor rejected. She has a problem to try to help this isolate become more acceptable to the group.

A Form for Recording the Results. A form for recording the replies may be adapted from the daily record sheet, or a new form may be prepared, which lists the pupils' names with six spaces after each name to record each choice. As a child is questioned, his choice should be written in the corresponding column opposite his name so that each child's selection will be immediately available for evaluation by the teacher.

Charting the Information. For the final charts, the teacher should number the names so that the records may be kept confidential. Symbols may be used for composing the charts. A simple form is the circle for the girls and a triangle for the boys. The chart should be numbered at the top of the page to identify the number of the question from the sociogram. A typical chart for question number three is shown with this chapter. It pictures the responses of fifteen children in one class of educable mentally retarded.

Evaluating the Information. The chart, or graph, as illustrated here and numbered three, indicates the question asked was, "Whom would you like for a partner in a game?" This chart shows that a boy, number 12, was chosen four times. He was the most popular of the pupils for this question. The reciprocal choices were 5 and 11; and 6 and 7. There were chain choices: 8 to 1; 1 to 12; 4 to 14; 10 to 9; 9 to 12; 12 to 11; 15 to 13; 13 to 12; 3 to 7. The ones who were not chosen were: 2, 4, 8, 10, and 15. This indicates at least five lonely children in the group of fifteen and much rivalry for the attention of child number 12.

The results of the sociogram may be shown in another way. The teacher may cut figures from colored paper or pictures from catalogs to represent the children. These figures or pictures may be pasted to a large cardboard on which colored lines may indicate the acceptance or rejection of each pupil. This method is shown in the accompanying illustration.

Utilizing the Information. It should be the teacher's duty to discover why these pupils were accepted or rejected and why one child was so well accepted. She will need much patience and tact to bring the rejected children into the group and help them to become better accepted. She must discover whether the cause of the rejection is health, personal hygiene, lack of skill in a game, or attitudes toward others. Whatever the cause of the rejection, the teacher should make every effort to help this child become acceptable.

The teacher may improve troubled spots in the classroom almost immediately by shifting the children's desks to different parts of the room. There is nothing to be gained by compelling two persons who actively dislike each other to sit side by side. Although children's habits are not quickly changed or formed, they may be gradually reformed by the teacher's patient, helpful direction into more desirable patterns.

A new sociogram may be given to the children when a problem is presented by unusual behavior. The questions should be changed in content to suit the conditions. Even if no problem appears, the teacher should give a sociogram several times during the year to compare the status of the pupils. A child who was previously considered a nonentity may mature socially and become a leader, while some other child may show many rejections. The teacher may avoid trouble among the pupils by recognizing these changes and by using skillful guidance and careful groupings for recitations and activities.

SUMMARY

The teacher may prepare and administer a sociogram to determine the inter-relationships of the pupils. She should utilize this information to secure better grouping in activities, better seating arrangements, and better general social relationships.

13

ARITHMETIC

ARITHMETIC FOR THE EDUCABLE MENTALLY RETARDED

THE educable mentally retarded child should be taught arithmetic when he has a need for it and when he has developed a readiness for it. This usually occurs when he has a mental age of six or seven years. The normal child is ready for numbers when he is six to seven years of age chronologically. The mentally retarded child will be much older chronologically than the normal child when he arrives at a readiness age. Besides mental age, mental and physical health are factors to be considered in determining the child's readiness for arithmetic.

Disabilities That Affect the Understanding of Arithmetic. The mentally retarded are severely handicapped in the study of arithmetic because of certain disabilities which have been discussed in detail in previous chapters. The following characteristics are especially applicable to the study of arithmetic: low transfer of learning; low abstract thinking ability; poor comprehension and observation of details and situations; slow absorption of facts; little initiative, and lack of ability to concentrate.

The Objectives in Teaching Arithmetic to the Educable Mentally Retarded. The teacher must face the above disabilities and plan methods to achieve objectives desirable for these children both for the present and for the future. The objectives should include teaching the essentials in arithmetic that will enable the person to preserve his personal diginity in ordinary business transactions.

The fundamental processes of arithmetic should be made automatic so that they are incidental in solving problems. Through

46. An Arithmetic Lesson.

the development of good work habits and a feeling of security in his ability to solve arithmetic problems, the pupils will develop independence and self-reliance in other areas.

Basis of the Program. The program must not be a "watered-down" version of a regular class, but one pared of non-essentials, devoted to basic skills and learnings. The teacher must build this program on lifelike situations and problems structured with oral problems for drill and fixing facts. These should be interspersed with simple written examples for practice that will facilitate accuracy and develop speed in using fundamental processes. Hence, it becomes a teaching situation involving an individual or a small group.

Readiness for Arithmetic. As with normal pupils, the mentally retarded must achieve a readiness and a mental age for a process before it is presented to them. Children in the regular primary room are in the process of acquiring readiness for numbers. This is developed through play activities, games, touching and handling materials, and directing class activities. The mentally retarded are given similar preparation, but it must be simplified, explained in detail, and continued for a longer period of time. Because of their mental age, many are still in the readiness stage when they are advanced to the intermediate group.

Intermediate Group Age Span. Children in the intermediate group are usually from 10 to 13 years of age chronologically. Their mental ages are from 4-5 to 8-6. The age for number readiness for the normal child, as previously listed, is 6-0 to 7-0 years chronologically. The age of 6 years and 6 months or even an older mental age is preferred by many teachers before starting number activities. The mentally retarded child should be at least that age mentally before he can be expected to have the understanding to make any growth in his ability to use numbers.

The basic skills are established and maintained during the three or four years the children remain in the intermediate group. The pupils will need these skills where they are advanced to the older group where they will have an opportunity for experiences in problems dealing with wages, jobs, installment buying, upkeep of a car and a home, trips, insurance, taxes, using banking facilities, writing orders for merchandise, managing an income, and taking care of household expenses.

Attention Span. Although a group of mentally retarded may work together for a short time, the best teaching is done individually. Most of the mentally retarded are easily distracted. They are unusually distractible when tired, angry, frustrated, or grouped with several other children. After the regular group work has been presented, the teacher should devote some time to each child. This individual help will develop greater understanding of a process than half an hour of group instruction.

Since the mentally retarded child's attention span is short and his interest wanes with each passing moment, the problem should be immediately explained and demonstrated. A new objective should be set up for the child, and he should be sent back to his seat to work.

Length of Drill. Five minutes is as long as the child's interest can be held in a drill on number facts. He should be given something else to do while the teacher works with another child. This whole program of training the educable mentally retarded for a useful life is a slow process which cannot be hurried.

Counting Devices, or "Crutches." "Crutches" in arithmetic refer to little methods and aids for working examples without memorizing facts. Some children count on their fingers; some make a series of dots; some make marks; others use beans or an abacus to arrive at an answer.

The child should be weaned from his need to count objects or fingers to find sums as soon as possible. He should be made to feel confident of his ability to recall the sums and differences between groups. If he continues to use "crutches," he will come to a plateau in his learning ability where he will be discouraged.

He will be unable to proceed when he is ready to begin working problems with columns of numbers in more difficult combinations. Before presenting new material the teacher should review until the child has a feeling of security. Since many of the mentally retarded will always need a "crutch" to solve even the simplest example, the use of supporting devices is better than not being able to move. Knowing how to add, subtract, multiply, and divide, even though relying heavily upon mechanical aids, is satisfying and useful to the child.

Making Numbers Meaningful. The teacher may utilize school situations to make numbers meaningful. This will help prepare the pupils for actual instruction in specific skills. She must take the time to explain every detail of a process, to drill on the facts, and to work for comprehension of number values.

The teacher must prepare many pages of examples for oral and written work. She must present the same facts and skills in many ways so that they may become workable concepts for the mentally retarded. Concrete objects—such as pennies, small blocks, books, or clothes pins—should be used first, followed by semi-concrete materials, such as pictures on cards, dots on cards, and finally the number symbol alone.

Limitations of the Regular Work Books. In preparing a program for the mentally retarded, one encounters difficulties in using a regular series of work books. These books were prepared for children with normal intelligence, who are able to use abstract ideas, to analyze a situation, and to use the reading vocabulary of a particular grade level. The teacher of the educable mentally retarded will be able to use some of the pages from many sets of work books. Teacher-made work sheets should be substituted for the too abstract and too difficult ones.

The Need for Repetition. The findings of the "Committee of Seven," as reported in the *Thirty-eighth Year Book of the National Society for the Study of Education,* shows that for the average person 67 repetitions were required to fix an easy addition combination; over 100, for a moderately difficult combination; and 150, for a difficult combination. The teacher of the mentally retarded should keep these facts in mind when preparing lesson plans. She should remember that perfecting skill in numbers takes patience and persistence.

Inventory of Ability. The teacher should take a semi-yearly inventory of the number ability of the children and start teaching where their understanding ends. If there seems to be a weakness, she should re-teach and review until there is a solid base from which to proceed. A check list is given in this chapter.

Types of Materials. As in all work with the mentally retarded, the simple approach is the most effective in the development of number concepts. The use of familiar materials for counting, such as blocks, buttons, spools, and the abacus, will not distract the children from the number lesson. The teacher should also provide simple play materials for the children who do not have the ability to proceed with the regular training program.

PROGRESS CHART AND CHECK LIST

Mental Age of 6-6 to 7-0. At a mental age of 6-6 to 7-0, the child should be ready to understand and to assimilate the following concepts:

Rote counting—1 through 5

Values of the numbers 1 through 5

Grouping—1, 2, 3

Writing numbers—1, 2, 3, 4, 5

Ordinal numbers—first, second

Meaning of terms—more than, last, and, put together, altogther, day, night

Addition—with no sum greater than 5

Subtraction—none

Sight recognition of the words *one,* and *two*

Time—meaning of o'clock, clock, hour

Money—one cent, 1c, 2c, 3c, 4c, 5c, nickel

Use of 1 and 2 in simple oral additive examples.

Recognition of a circle

Calendar—practice in locating the day of the week and the date of the month.

Recognition of the signs + and =, for *and* and *equals.*

Measurement—cup, teaspoon, tablespoon, dozen

Methods—Arith.

All of the above should be completely mastered before proceeding to the next steps in arithmetic.

Mental Age of 7-0 to 7-6. At a mental age of 7-0 to 7-6, the child should be ready to understand and to assimilate the following concepts:

Rote counting—6 through 10
Grouping—1, 2, 3, 4, 5
Writing numbers—6, 7, 8, 9, 10
Ordinal numbers—third, fourth
Meaning of terms—take away, less, subtract, plus
Addition—with no sum greater than 10
Subtraction—presentation of the facts from 1 through 5 as a unit; then the presentation of the facts from 6 through 10, parallel with each new addition fact.
Sight recognition of the words *three, four,* and *five.*
Time—half-hour, afternoon, morning, evening, noon; counting the hours to 10
Money—dime, 10c, making change from 1c through 10c
Recognition of the square, and of the sign − for take away or subtract.
Calendar—days of the week, the date, the weather
Zero—as a place holder
Measurement—pint, inch, half-dozen, ½ of each, ½ of a group up to 10
Child's telephone number and street address

Mental Age 7-6 to 8-0. At a mental age of 7-6 to 8-0, the child should be ready to understand and to assimilate the following concepts:

Rote counting—1 through 50
Values of the numbers 1 through 50
Grouping—easy addition and subtraction facts
Counting by decades—10 through 50
Writing numbers—1 through 50
Ordinal numbers—fifth, sixth
Meaning of terms—tens, teens, ones, units, 30 minutes
Addition—simple oral and written examples with sums of 19 or less
Subtraction—simple oral and written examples with remainders of 19 or less

Sight recognition of the words five, six
Time—minute, counting of minutes from 1 through 50
Money—quarter, 25c, making change to 25c
Recognition of a triangle
Calendar—days of week, date, weather report
Zero—as a place holder
Measurement—quart, foot, 12 inches, ¼ of each, ¼ of a group

Mental Age 8-0 to 8-6. At a mental age of 8-0 to 8-6 the child should understand and be ready to assimilate the following concepts:

Rote counting—50 through 100
Values of the numbers 50 through 100
Grouping—more difficult addition and subtraction facts
Counting by decades—50 through 100
Counting by 5's—5 through 50
Counting by 2's—2 through 10
Writing numbers—1 through 100
Ordinal numbers—seventh, eighth
Meaning of terms—review
Addition—more difficult addition facts, simple oral and written examples with no carrying, one-place column of three numbers with no sum over 10
Subtraction—more difficult subtraction facts, simple oral and written examples with no borrowing
Sight recognition of the words seven and eight.
Time—quarter hour, 15 minutes, days of the week, date, midnight, A. M.
Money—half-dollar, 50c, making change for 50c
Recognition of a rectangle or oblong
Calendar—day of the week, date of the month, the month, the year, the weather record
Measurement—yard, 3 feet, 36 inches, ⅓ of each, ⅓ of a group
Place values in numbers—ones, tens, hundreds

Mental Age of 8-6 to 9-0. At a mental age of 8-6 to 9-0, the child should be ready to understand and to assimilate the following concepts:

Counting—100's to 500

Counting—5's to 100; 2's to 50; 3's to 21
Reading and writing numbers—1 to 500
Ordinal numbers—ninth, tenth
Meaning of terms—review; times, multiply, multiplication
Addition—two-place numbers in examples with no carrying, single column examples with no sum over 10, simple oral situation examples
Subtraction—two-place numbers in examples with no borrowing, simple oral situation examples with no remainder over 10
Sight recognition of words—nine and ten
Time—month, names of months, 12 months in a year, days of week, date, hour, minute, second
Money—one dollar, $ for dollar, $1.00, decimal . sign, making change for one dollar, reading money in dollars and cents
Calendar—day of week, date of month, the year, weather record
Measurement—city block, mile
Place values in numbers—ones or units, tens, hundreds, thousands
Multiplication—the two's and the sign X for times or for multiply

Mental Age of 9-0 to 10-6. At a mental age of 9-0 to 10-6, the child should be ready to understand and to assimilate the following concepts:

Reading, writing numbers—to 1,000
Addition—100 facts; problems with no carrying
Subtraction—100 facts; problems with no borrowing
Multiplication—1's, 2's, 3's, 4's, 5's; simple problems with no carrying
Problems—simple familiar situations
Examples—two- and three-place numbers
Division—simple examples with one- and two-place numbers
Recognition of signs—division signs— ⟌, ÷
Ordinal numbers—auditory familiarity with tenth through twentieth
Cardinal number names—sight recognition—one through twenty
Time—365 days in a year, 7 days in a week, 52 weeks in a year, names of holidays, names of months in a year
Money—five dollars, $5.00, ten dollars, $10.00, making change to ten dollars

Measurement—2 pints equal 1 quart, 12 inches equal 1 foot, 3 feet equal 1 yard, 16 ounces equal 1 pound
Abbreviations—qt., lb., yd., in., pt.
Thermometer—telling temperature
Scales—reading pounds and ounces
Recognition of a cube, a cylinder, and a sphere.
Reading and writing Roman numerals from I to X.

TEACHING NUMBER CONCEPTS

Methods for Rote Counting. When the child has attained the mental age of 6-6 to 7-0, he should have achieved a readiness for understanding numbers. At this time the teacher may begin presenting rote counting. Number rhymes are good for this purpose. New pupils or those with readiness will enjoy participating in the singing and easy choral readings. The more mature children, who also enjoy rhymes, will help the others to learn them.

The children may sing "Ten Little Indians," then dramatize it. The child who is starting to learn the meaning of number may be at the head of the line. He may be named **One.** As the children sing the song and name the numbers, **Child One** will step forward and then back into place in the line. As the children sing about the number two, **Child One** takes the hand of the child next to him and they step forward. Both children step back into line as the song proceeds.

The teacher must be careful to emphasize the idea of *one,* the group of *two,* or the group of *three,* to show the values of *one, two,* and *three.* She must not allow the children to confuse the number values with ordinal values of *first, second,* or *third* places. Following are some examples of old nursery rhymes and finger plays with simple directions that may be used to help teach the values of numbers. The teacher leads the rhymes and indicates the values and the actions.

One for the Money

One for the money, (Hold up one finger.)
Two for the show, (Hold up two fingers.)
Three to make ready, (Hold up three fingers.)
Four to go. (Hold up four fingers.)

—*Anonymous*

Hickory, Dickory, Dock!

Hickory, Dickory, Dock!
(Raise the left arm over the head to represent a tall clock.)
The mouse ran up the clock;
(Raise right hand and imitate a mouse running up the clock.)
The clock struck one, and down he ran.
(Clap hands as *one* is said.)
Hickory, Dickory, Dock!

—*Mother Goose*

Two Little Blackbirds

Two little blackbirds sitting on a hill.
(Close fists, thumbs up.)
One named Jack and one named Jill,
(Waggle thumbs.)
Fly away, Jack! (Move right hand behind back.)
Fly away, Jill! (Move left hand behind back.)
Come back, Jack! (Bring right hand in front.)
Come back Jill! (Bring left hand in front.)
Two little blackbirds siting on a hill,
(Closed fists with thumbs up, bobbing in front of child.)
One named Jack and one named Jill. (Waggle thumbs.)

—*Mother Goose*

Two Little Blackbirds may also be played as a game with a boy and a girl taking the parts of the birds, Jack and Jill. They may act out the movements of Jack and Jill as the rhyme is repeated. The *two* value is more evident when the rhyme is dramatized in this manner than when using it as a finger play.

Five Little Squirrels

Five little squirrels sitting in a tree,
(Hold left hand up, fingers limp from the wrist.)
This little squirrel says, "What do I see?"
(Begin with thumb and hold up a finger as each squirrel is named.)
This little squirrel says, "I see a gun."
This little squirrel says, "Let us run."
This little squirrel says, "I'm not afraid."
This little squirrel says, "Let's hide in the shade."
Along came a man with a great big gun.
(Right hand moves up as finger points in imitation of a gun.)
Bang! See those little squirrels run.
(Clap hands and hide left hand.)

—*Anonymous*

The above rhyme may also be used as instructional material for teaching the ordinals by substituting *first* through *fifth* for the word *this* at the beginning of each line.

Mother Hen and Chickens

(Point to each finger to indicate the *first, second, third,* etc., as the rhyme is repeated.)

Said the first little chicken with a queer little squirm,
"I wish I could find a nice fat worm."
Said the second little chicken with an odd little shrug,
"I wish I could find a nice fat bug."
Said the third little chicken with a sigh of relief,
"I wish I could find a nice green leaf."
Said the fourth little chicken with a queer little squeal,
"I wish I could find some nice yellow meal."
"Now see here," said the mother hen from the green garden patch,
"If you want any breakfast, come here and scratch."

—*Unknown*

Grouping of Numbers. Grouping consists of arranging all of the possible combinations of numbers whose sums equal a given amount, as in the combinations 1 and 4; 2 and 3; 4 and 1; 3 and 2; the sums all equal 5. The concept of each number in the series of one through five with all of the grouping combinations should be presented parallel with the teaching of rote counting.

Many of the rhymes used as choral readings will assist the children in understanding the real meaning of numbers. However, there must be many other activities to fix the concept of the value of the numbers: how its place in the number system is related to the numbers before and after it; whether it is larger or smaller; between which numbers it occurs; how it is composed of various groupings; and in turn how it is part of another number.

Using Concrete Materials. Concrete materials are those which may be actually used by the child to make definite problems. These may be clocks, buttons, sticks, blocks, or any objects that are easy to handle. The use of this type of material helps to structure the meaning for the child. The muscular activity used in touching, lifting, pushing, and moving objects contribute immeasurably to the retention of the idea of the value of a number.

Teaching the Concept of One. A method of presenting the idea of *one* is to give directions to the children, using the term at every opportunity. A sample follows:

Move one chair away from the table.
Bring one sheet of paper to the desk.
Give one pencil to Sue.
Give each pupil one napkin.

Blocks are useful in presenting an activity of this type. They should be large enough to handle easily, but not too bulky for grouping. Blocks of the same color are suitable for this kind of instruction. The teacher directs the children's play as follows:

Pick up one block. Lay it on the table.
Give Tom one block.
Sue, take one block out of the box.
Bill, I will give you one block.
James, give one block to Sue.

Each child should be encouraged to reply, "One block," or "Here is one block." In the beginning of the drill the teacher should not suggest complete sentences in response to her directions; but wait until the number concept is established. Thinking of the correct sentence form might so frustrate the child that he would be unable to answer the basic question.

The teacher should contrive variations of the play with the blocks. She should use dolls, pennies, books, marbles, chalk, crayons, or any familiar objects available in the room. When the child has a concept of the number value and is familiar with the oral name of the number, the visual symbol may be presented for sight recognition.

Presenting the Symbol for One. The teacher may find some of the following suggestions helpful in presenting the cardinal number 1:

Draw the symbol 1 on the chalkboard.
Make the line thick and several inches long.
Give the child a piece of chalk. Help him to make the symbol 1.
He should practice making the number and repeat the name for it as he draws.
The teacher should help him make the 1 on paper with a pencil.
He should use a pencil with a soft lead.
Give the child a stencil form or a plastic number 1 to trace around, and then let him color the pattern he has drawn.
Draw the number 1 on clay in the clay pan and let the child use a stylus to trace over it.
He should repeat the name, *one*, as he traces.
Draw the number 1 on cardboard or heavy drawing paper with different colors of crayon.
Clip tracing paper to the page and let the child trace the numbers with the same colors of crayons as the original while he repeats name of the symbol, *one*.

Training the Auditory Sense. Understanding of the number values may be intensified by the teacher's use of auditory training: clap the hands; sound a bell; tap on the desk; sound a note on the piano, at the same time naming the action or object in connection with the number being presented to the child.

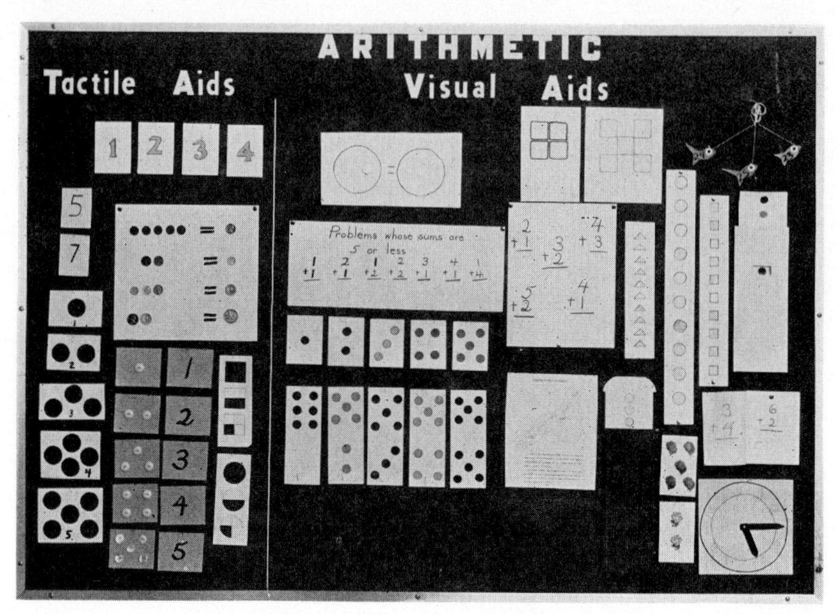

47. Tactile and visual aids.

Using Semiconcrete Materials. Materials classified as semiconcrete are such things as pictures, dots or simple marks on cards. The flash cards should be white or buff with blue or black dots about an inch across for quick recognition. After three dots have been used on the cards, dots that are too small or too large are confusing. The child is better able to form a mental image if the dots are arranged in a domino pattern which will assist him in grouping and in computing accurately and more rapidly.

Clear, distinct pictures should be used for flash cards. There should be nothing to distract from the idea of the value of the 1, 2, or 3. A picture should leave no doubt in the child's mind that this means one cat, one dog, two fish, or three apples.

If a fish picture is used, there should be no part of a fish line showing. The fish should neither be shown on a dish, nor be held by someone. Pictures of two dogs must be identical. A picture of a dog and a cat would be confusing. The child would say," A dog and a cat." He would not usually respond, "Two animals." The mentally retarded child would see one dog and one cat. This necessitates cutting out all extraneous matter, without mutilating

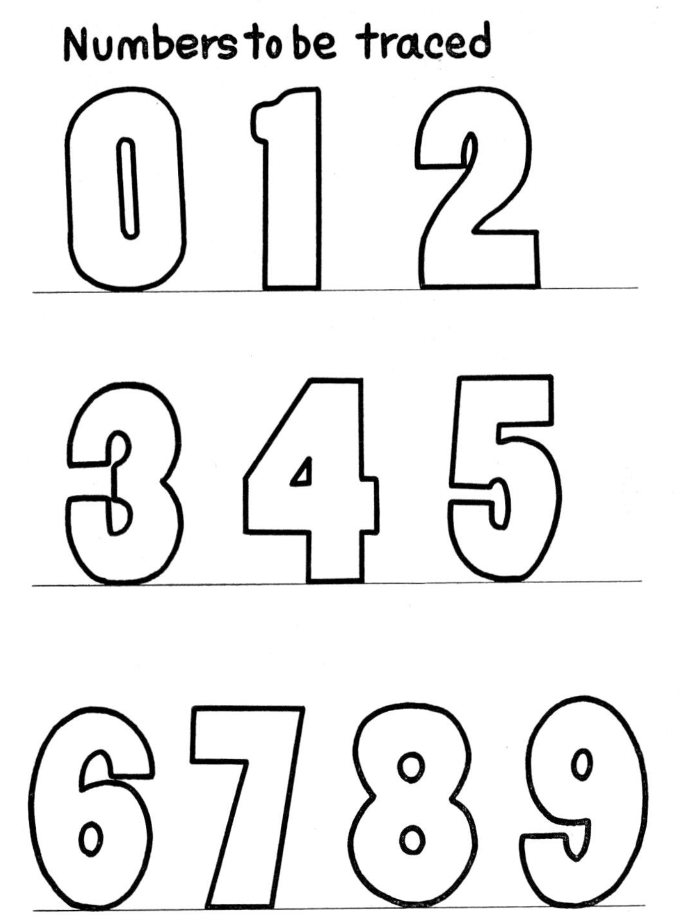

48. Stimulating the visual memory for numerals.

the picture. In groups of such pictures as five apples, each apple should be identical, with the pictures of the apples arranged in domino pattern.

The following directions may be of assistance to the teacher in presenting semiconcrete materials to the pupils: Show the child a card with one dot on it. Say, "One." The child should pick up the card and repeat, "One."

Take a card from the child and say, "One dot." The child should repeat, "One dot." Put the card with other cards having more than one dot on them. Instruct the child to find the one dot card. When he finds it, he repeats, "One dot." If he does not remember the one dot from more than one dot, go over the cards again as before.

Use the same routine for pictures on flash cards. The child must give back verbally the exact information the teacher has given him in order to fix the concept in his mind. This can be accomplished only through dozens of repetitions.

Stimulating the Visual Memory for Numerals. Children enjoy coloring large numerals. These should be dittoed, as the children will use many of them. The numbers should be large enough to be outlined first with a crayon and then colored solidly. The child should say the name of the number as he colors it.

A stencil should be cut from heavy cardboard for the use of any child who has trouble staying inside the lines. He should use a black pencil or crayon; then when he lifts the stencil the number is outlined and heavily colored so that he can see its correct shape.

Numbers cut from emery paper and pasted to cards are used for training the tactile sense. The child lightly traces over the number with his forefinger as if writing the number. He repeats the name of the number as he traces over it.

While the child is learning the concept of *one*, he may be given a page of all of the numerals to trace around and to color. At this time no attempt is made to teach him the names of the other numerals. He is merely becoming familiar with their shapes. However, as he participates in activities, he will become aware of the names of the other numerals.

Presenting Subtraction After Addition. In presenting the meaning of subtraction, the teacher should wait until after the concept of the sums of the numbers whose addends equals five or less is firmly established.

Teaching the Concept of Two. As confidence increases and the child uses *one* with meaning, *two* may be introduced in the same manner as *one* was presented. The teacher should use the same materials and proceed through the same steps. She will insist that the child repeat the name of the numerals with the name of the object or action, such as two blocks, two dots, two marbles, two bounces of the ball. This precaution will prevent a fixation that connects any number with an object. Numerical songs, number games, and choral games will also emphasize the number being taught.

Presenting One and One Are Two. When the child can recognize two objects and can pick two things out of a group, he is ready to be made aware that *one and one are two.* This is accomplished with objects, little oral examples and problems, and finally with numbers on the chalkboard. At this time the children may be shown the sign for plus, and told to call it *and.*

Column addition is easier for the children to understand than the equation form. After they become familiar with column addition, the equation form is presented. Also, one-place column addition with three numbers should be taught parallel with grouping as well as the combinations of numbers whose sums are equal to or less than three.

The child should be shown how to make the equals sign. He must practice writing an example and reading it aloud many times, to become familiar with the form and content. He will learn how to write it and how to read it only after a long period of instruction. This stage in arithmetic is a great achievement for the mentally retarded. After practice on the combination *one and one are two,* the teacher may present the same example in column form again and continue the drill.

The examples may be scattered in irregular form over the page with a large space left around each one to break up the tendency of the child to skip or to do only one example. Only three to five examples should be used to a page at first. Crayons or a felt-tipped pen may be used to make the large numbers all of one color. The child should write the answers with a different color crayon. This allows him to see his progress.

Teaching the First Ordinal. The child is now ready to have the meaning of the ordinal *first* demonstrated. Stand several children in a single file facing the front of the room. Ask, "Who is first?" Some of the children may know the answer. If not, indicate the one who is *first* in the line.

Move another child up to first place and ask the same question. Have each child turn around in place and face the back of the room. Ask, "Who is first in line?" Touch the child who is the first one in line to be sure the group understands the meaning of the word.

Use objects in the same manner to continue the teaching of the meaning of the term *first.* Place in rows; books, toys, pennies, blocks, pictures, buttons, or crayons. Ask the child to touch the first block in a row and to say, "This is the first block."

After each child is confident of the pronunciation of the word *first* and of its correct use, he should make a complete sentence and say, "This is the first block in the row."

Teaching the Meaning of Last. The concept of *last* should be presented after the teaching of *first.* Use the same procedure as for teaching the concept of *first.*

Teaching the Ordinals, Second Through Tenth. There must be a delay of several months between teaching the meaning of the different ordinals in order that the concept may be thoroughly assimilated and made useable.

Teaching Three. When the child knows the values of *one* and *two,* present *three* in the same detailed manner. Associate the number with concrete objects, but vary the material from day to day so that the child will not be convinced that it is only when he picks up purple spools that he has *three.*

The concept of three is so much more difficult than that of one or two for the child to understand that it will take much longer for him to assimilate the meaning, and it will necessitate many more presentations. A variety of objects may be collected by the children and used by the teacher to stimulate interest and understanding in counting. These objects, which should be kept within a size range that lend themselves readily to grouping and handling, may include spools, beads, beans, corn, blocks, buttons, acorns, pumpkin and sunflower seeds, or small boxes.

Testing for Readiness for a New Concept. The child now knows the oral and written forms for 1, 2, and 3. He recognizes or selects 1, 2, or 3 objects as directed. Now the teacher should particularly observe the child's ability to understand these groups by reversing the order of the groups before advancing to the next number.

There are maturity levels of comprehension for the numerical values of a group of objects. Unless the child has the readiness for this process, it is useless to try to force comprehension.

Introducing Oral and Written Examples. When the child is able to comprehend the values of *one* and *two* and can make the written symbols, give him written examples for seat work along with little oral problems in class. Then, as comprehension develops for the number *three,* increase the range of examples. The child will need drill to establish procedures for working the examples and fixing the facts so that they will be automatic. Start this drill at the chalkboard, where every move of the child can be easily studied. Give him confidence by showing him how to do the work.

After the pupil has attained some confidence at the chalkboard, give him a page of examples. Sit by him often to help him establish good work habits. Teach the child to work from the left to the right on the page. He must learn to solve the first example in the first row on the page. He must learn to solve the second problem, and then the third one in order, and to continue on row after row until he solves the last example on the page.

Teaching the Word Add. The teacher should write the word *Add* on the chalkboard. Let the child practice it on the board. Then write *Add* on paper for the child to copy. Later use the word in drills with the addition facts and with the signs used in addition.

Preparing Examples for Beginners. The teacher should prepare the examples with a primary-sized pencil, felt-tipped pen, or crayon, so that the numerals are large and the signs are easily distinguished. Careful numeral formation is important. Nine to fifteen examples to a sheet, staggered and widely spread, is about right at this stage of ability for the pupil.

Many pupils are bewildered or frustrated by receiving a page closely covered with examples. Since the task looks formidable, they give up before starting. Sometimes a child will work only one example on the page. The teacher may outwit him by putting one example on a page. When he works the one example, she must praise him and write another one for him to work.

This is very trying for the teacher if she has a full case load

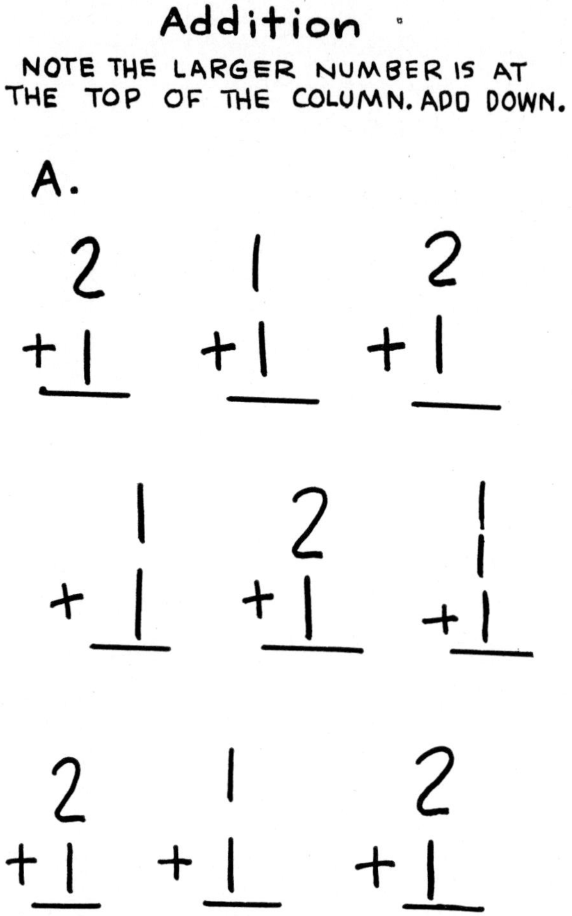

Addition

NOTE THE LARGER NUMBER IS AT THE TOP OF THE COLUMN. ADD DOWN.

A.

$$\begin{array}{r}2\\+1\\\hline\end{array}\quad\begin{array}{r}1\\+1\\\hline\end{array}\quad\begin{array}{r}2\\+1\\\hline\end{array}$$

$$\begin{array}{r}1\\+1\\\hline\end{array}\quad\begin{array}{r}2\\+1\\\hline\end{array}\quad\begin{array}{r}1\\1\\+1\\\hline\end{array}$$

$$\begin{array}{r}2\\+1\\\hline\end{array}\quad\begin{array}{r}1\\+1\\\hline\end{array}\quad\begin{array}{r}2\\+1\\\hline\end{array}$$

49. Addition examples for beginners.

of children in the room. Sometimes the child will accept a page of examples that has been folded into strips. Each strip is completed before the next one is unfolded.

Another method of handling this type of situation is to fold a paper into squares and to write an example on each square. The paper may be cut along the folds, and one example at a time may be given to the child. The examples should be collected as they are completed. When working with a group, the teacher may allow each child to keep his material in a box on his desk. This procedure will eliminate unnecessary movement around the room.

In preparing the examples, the teacher at first should use the larger number at the top and teach the child to add down the column. After the sum of the combination is fixed in the child's consciousness, the other corresponding fact may be included in the sets of examples.

Teaching the Place of a Number in a Series. The child must be taught to recognize that each number in the series has a special place and meaning. This may be accomplished by using objects placed in rows to show that a number is one more than the number it precedes and that it is one less than the number after it.

The give-and-take of dialogue between the teacher and the child is important for retention and eventual comprehension. The teacher may use a procedure similar to the following, using buttons, beans, blocks or cards to illustrate the problem: In the sample dialogue, **T** represents the teacher and **C** represents the child.

T: Two are more than one. Place one button beside another button.
Take away the button.

C: Two are more than one.

Repeat this procedure over and over, using many kinds of objects. Use sticks to demonstrate.

T: I will give you one stick. How many sticks do you have?

C: One stick.

T: Here is one more stick. Put this stick with your other stick. Now I will pick up a stick. Do you have more sticks than I have?

C: I have more sticks.

T: How many sticks do you have?

C: Two sticks.

T: Now, you tell me that two sticks are more than one stick.

C: Two sticks are more than one stick.

Repeat this type of drill over and over, changing the objects so that the child will not associate the *more than* with any one object. At the same time, the teacher should try to get the child to give a complete sentence as a response to her question.

2 +1   1 +1   2 +1

2 + 1=   1+1=
1 + 1=   2+1=
2 + 1=   1+1=

2 +1   1 +1   2 +1

2 +1   1 +2   1 1 +1

1 + 2   1 +1   2 +1
2 + 1
1 + 1   1 +2   1 1 +1
1 + 1 + 1
2 + 1 =

1 +2   1 +1   2 +1

2+1=   2+1=
1+1=   1+2=
1+2=   1+1=
1+1=   1+1+1=

2 +1   1 +2   1 +1   1 1 +1

2 + 1=   2 +1   1 +2
1 + 2 =
1 + 1 1 =
1 + 1 =

1 1 1   1 +2   2 +1   1 +1

50. Introducing the equation form of addition.

When the child is ready for another number in the series, the same procedure is carried out. The concept of *less* should not be taught parallel with *more than* at this time, as it would confuse the child. Only after the concept of the numbers 1, 2, 3, 4, and 5 have been established should the idea of *less than* be presented.

Teaching the Concept of Second. The procedure for teaching the concept of *second* is similar to that of presenting *first.* Review the ordinal *first.* Place the children in rows; sing the number

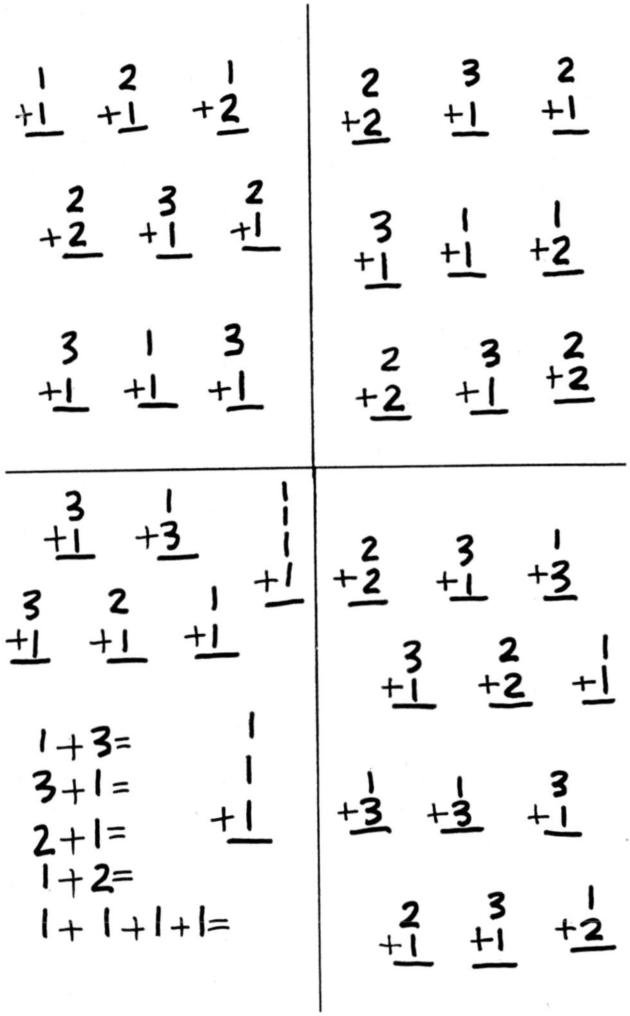

51. Introducing partial counting.

songs; use blocks, marbles, and buttons; ask the children questions and let them echo the answers until there seems to be an understanding of the term *second.*

T: Give the second block to me.

C: Here is the second block.

These basic concepts cannot be hurried. The presentation of this simple material will consume weeks of time. The teacher must remember that the material, the objects, and the flash cards with pictures must be varied continuously to hold interest and to prevent the child from associating meaning with material.

Teaching Grouping and Partial Counting. When the child is ready mentally to understand grouping and partial counting, he will be able to recognize two objects and associates them with the name *two*. However, the child may be able to use the word *two* without knowing the meaning of the number two. He may revert to counting each object as he has not had enough drill on the recognition of groups before he begins to combine the groups.

Partial counting begins with naming the first number in a series without tapping or using counters, and continues from there to arrive at the sum, such as 4 and 2 are 6. Later he may be able to give the sum of 6 without counting out the last numbers. The child should be weaned of the habit of saying, "1, 2, 3, 4, and 5, 6," for 4 and 2 are 6.

Partial counting practice should begin with the previously mastered concepts of 1, 2, and 3 and be continued until they are automatic with the child. Then the numbers 4 and later 5 are presented. At this stage, partial counting is limited to the combinations taught and does not include other groupings. If the child is hurried too fast for his mental ability or if he has a lack of confidence, he may manifest a reversion by using counters.

Aiding the Retention of Facts. Assimilation of the facts is accomplished so slowly by some children that it may be necessary to permit them to use counters in the manner of beginners, so that they may solve problems and have a feeling of success. Continued drill in competency would do more harm to the personality than the gain in skill would warrant. Examples should be prepared within the limits of the numbers formerly taught and upon which the children have been drilled.

Using the Flannel Board. Another way to vary the presentation of the lessons is to use the flannel board. This is effective in teaching number groups or the meaning of numbers. A flannel board is inexpensive to make and limitless in its use.

The base of the flannel board may be a piece of heavy cardboard with a cover of heavy outing flannel or felt stretched over it.

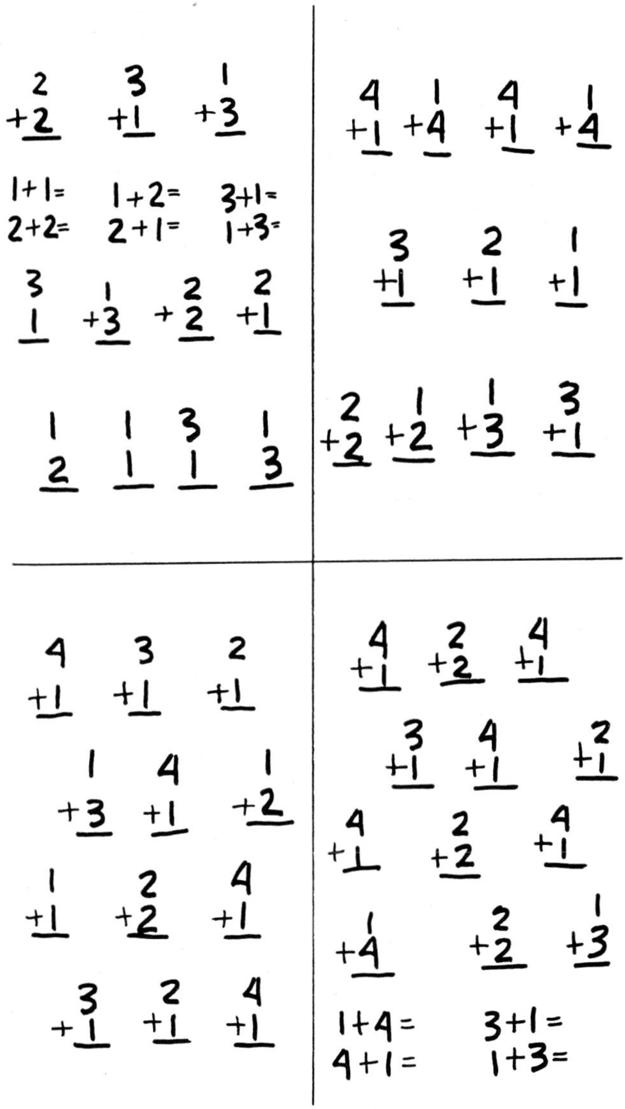

2 3 1
+2 +1 +3

1+1= 1+2= 3+1=
2+2= 2+1= 1+3=

3 1 2 2
1 +3 +2 +1

1 1 3 1
2 1 1 3

4 1 4 1
+1 +4 +1 +4

3 2 1
+1 +1 +1

2 1 1 3
+2 +2 +3 +1

4 3 2
+1 +1 +1

1 4 1
+3 +1 +2

1 2 4
+1 +2 +1

3 2 4
+1 +1 +1

4 2 4
+1 +2 +1

3 4 2
+1 +1 +1

4 2 4
+1 +2 +1

1 2 1
+4 +2 +3

1+4= 3+1=
4+1= 1+3=

52. Introducing grouping.

The flannel is sewed across the back of the cardboard to keep it smooth and taut. White or black outing flannel is the best background for presenting numbers.

Circles may be cut from heavy flannel or from old felt hats of a contrasting color. These circles cling to the flannel board, yet they are easily moved about for grouping in teaching addition and subtraction.

The domino pattern should be used consistently in arranging the circles on the flannel board. Only the numerals the child has been prepared to understand through the previous use of concrete materials should be presented.

After this preparation flash cards with the numerals may be used for a visual recognition drill. The teacher may use domino patterns of dots or squares for the semi-concrete problems. No decorated objects should be pasted on the flash cards, as they detract from the number group.

Matching Exercises. The teacher may prepare matching exercises for the children by drawing large numbers on mimeographed sheets of paper. The children match the numbers by drawing lines between the similar symbols with crayons. The numbers may be written on heavy cardboard, over which tracing paper is clipped. The children draw lines on the tracing paper to match the similar numbers.

Another method for matching is that of using shoe-laces attached to the side of a plywood form on which the numbers and objects are painted. Holes are drilled into the plywood along the other side of the board into which the laces are strung as the numbers and objects are matched.

As each numeral is learned, it should be added to the list of numbers to be matched with objects. Matching may be used as a review. Place number flash cards on a table with groups of objects. Ask the children to match the cards to the groups. Also use picture flash cards or domino cards to match the objects or the numbers.

The mentally retarded child dislikes to do the same exercises over and over. Since he soon recognizes the same sheet of examples, re-arrange the same material by using different pictures and designs. *Keep the materials simple.*

Teaching Number by Playing Games. Games are excellent to intensify learning and to assist in a socializing program. The use of games provides a practical experience in using number values. Change the points to be scored to suit the ability of the children, as in these games: beanbag, ringtoss, shuffleboard, hopscotch, or tenpins.

Make bean bags from any heavy material which can be sewed into bags about six inches square. Fill each one with six ounces of dried beans, which is the right weight for indoor use. Label shoe boxes and place them in a row as targets for the bean bags. Thumbtack the boxes to a piece of plywood so they will not slide about when the bags are tossed into them.

For beginners in counting, use *one box* for the bags to be tossed into. Label it 1. The players keep score by putting colored counting sticks beside their names. Each child should have sticks all of one color. Until the children are able to keep score, the teacher must count the sticks.

Make ten pins from round cereal boxes and paint them bright colors. Use a soft rubber ball to roll against the pins. Use as many pins as the children in the games are able to count. Start with one pin, if necessary, and add more as the children's counting ability increases. Keep scores with colored sticks as in the game of bean bag.

A toilet plunger makes a good peg for a ring toss game. The rings may be fruit jar rings, or they may be from short lengths of clothes line.

Teaching Tallying by Fives. The large sticks used for primary counting are excellent for teaching tallying by fives to the more advanced pupils who have learned to count by fives. Use the sticks instead of making pencil marks.

Using the abacus. The abacus may also be used for scoring after the children are mature enough to understand how to manipulate it.

Teaching the Words One and Two. Sight recognition of the words *one* and *two* may be taught as the child become proficient in the use of the addition combinations whose sums are five or less. Use the words as reading vocabulary. Write them on flash cards for matching with numbers, dots, or groups of objects.

2 − 1 3 − 1 4 − 1	2 − 1 3 − 1 4 − 1
5 − 1 3 − 2	5 − 1 2 − 1 3 − 1
5 − 4 2 − 1 4 − 3	4 − 1 2 − 1 5 − 1

2 − 1 3 − 2 4 − 1 5 − 1	1 + 1 2 − 1 2 + 1 1 + 2
3 − 1 5 − 4 4 − 3 2 − 1	3 − 1 3 − 2 3 + 1 1 + 3
5 − 1 4 − 1 3 − 1 2 − 1	4 − 1 4 − 3 4 + 1 1 + 4
5 − 4 4 − 3 3 − 2 2 − 1	5 − 1 5 − 4

53. Subtraction examples with some addition examples.

Subtraction-Mixed

4	2	1	3	0	4
−0	−1	−1	−0	−0	−4

$2-1=$ $2-0=$ $2-2=$

$1-1=$ $1-1=$ $0-0=$

$3-0=$ $4-4=$ $5-0=$

$3-3=$ $4-1=$ $5-5=$

$3-1=$ $4-0=$ $5-1=$

54. Sample examples for practice in column and equation form in subtraction.

Teaching Subtraction. Introduction to subtraction takes place *after* the complete presentation and understanding of the numbers 1 through 5. Introduce the minus sign as *take away.* This is an easily understood term and one with which the child is usually familiar. Present the numbers concretely, beginning with 2 and proceeding through the number series, 2 take away 1, to 5 take away 1. Zero is not presented at this time.

Present every step just as in addition, going from objects to the semiconcrete pictures and dots, and then to the number symbols. Give oral examples and problems first and then the worksheets of numbers to be subtracted.

2 3 4
-1 -1 -1

5 3
-1 -2

5 2 4
+4 -1 -3

2 3 4
-1 -1 -1

5 2 3
-1 -1 -1

4 2 5
-1 -1 -1

2 3 4 5
1 2 1 1

3 5 4 2
-1 -4 -3 -1

5 4 3 2
-1 -1 -1 -1

5 4 3 2
-4 -3 -2 -1

1 2 2 1
+1 -1 +1 +2

3 3 3 1
-1 -2 +1 +3

4 4 4 1
-1 -3 +1 +4

5 5
-1 -4

55. Sample examples–A, B, C, subtraction with no remainder greater than 4 and no zeros; D, addition and subtraction with no answer greater than 5 and no zeros.

ZERO IN REMAINDERS

1 2 3 4 5 0

-1 -2 -3 -4 -5 -0

ZERO IN THE SUBTRAHEND

1 2 3 4 5

-0 -0 -0 -0 -0

6 7 8 9

-0 -0 -0 -0

USING ZERO IN SUBTRACTION

2 3 4 1 2

-0 -0 -4 -0 -2

5 1 3 4

-5 -1 -3 -0

56. Using zero in subtraction.

2	2	1	3	4	5
-1	-2	-1	-2	-1	-1
5	3	5	2	4	5
-5	-1	-4	-0	-2	-3
4	1	5	2	4	3
-0	-0	-2	-2	-3	-3
5	3	0	4	5	5
-2	-0	-0	-4	-5	-0

57. Practice sheet in subtraction.

Assimilating Each Combination. Work on one combination at a time until it is assimilated into the child's memory with a concept of its meaning. Review the addition facts continuously as the corresponding subtraction facts are being taught. As each subtraction fact is established for the child, give practice pages with the corresponding addition facts. This is a tedious process for the teacher, but it is of great value to the child.

Presenting Zero in Remainders. Introduce zero as a remainder after the children understand subtraction facts whose remainders do not exceed four. These will need separate drill and must be taught as carefully as the preceding combinations. Proceed with the same methods and with step-by-step demonstrations with objects, then pictures, dots, and, at last, the number symbols.

4 3 2
+1 +1 +1

3+1= 2+1= 4+1=
4+1= 4+1= 3+1=
2+1= 3+1= 2+1=
4+1= 4+1= 4+1=

3 4 1
+1 +1 +1

1 1 1
+4 +3 +2

1 1 1
+1 +4 +3

4 4 1
+1 +1 +4

1 1 1
+1 +3 +2

4 1 4
+1 +4 +1

3 1 2
+1 +3 +1

1 1 2
+2 +1 +2

4 3 2
+1 +1 +1

4 3 2
+1 +1 +2

4 + 1=
1 + 4=
2 + 2=
1 + 2=
2 + 1=
3 + 1=
1 + 3=
1 + 1=

1
+4

3 1
+1 -1

1
+3

1
+2

58. Practice sheet for addition—no sum greater than 5.

Teaching the Value of Zero in the Subtrahend. The use of zero in the subtrahend should be taught with the same detail and care as in the preceding items, with objects, semiconcrete materials and the number symbols. Explain and dramatize every step to show the value of zero. The teacher should prepare many series of examples illustrating all possible combinations in the use of zero for the pupils' practice worksheets.

Teaching Grouping in Numbers 2 Through 5. The educable mentally retarded find it difficult to associate the relationships of numbers and to break numbers down into groups within a number. When the numbers have been thoroughly understood in their basic relationships of zero through five, it is important to start there with grouping and partial counting. Objects may be used to show the children all of the possible groups in each number. Then allow the pupils to write the group names as they recognize them. They should handle the groups of objects and talk about them.

Prepare practice sheets to review the previous instruction in partial counting. Try to proceed slowly so the child will have confidence in his ability to name the sums. After the grouping idea has been established for the addition combinations, take up the subtraction facts. Demonstrate with objects for every group and continue drill on the combinations until the child can work them. This will include many, many lessons and many practice sheets.

Arousing the Child's Interest in Number. Interest and the will to accomplish a given goal is important in all areas of learning. The child needs adequate preparation, as well as maturation, to achieve this goal. Careful spacing of new steps will aid in the progress of the child.

Everyday situations should be used to impress the child with the necessity of knowing the fact being presented. The teacher must continuously question the children about experiences involving number to make them realize that number is an important part of daily living.

Introducing More Difficult Games. As the child advances in number recognition and ability to group and to count, he will

3	5	1	6	6	4
+3	+1	+5	+1	−5	+4

6	1	7	7	7	5	7
+1	+6	−1	−1	−6	+5	+1

1	8	8	8	1	9
+7	−1	−7	+1	+8	−1

9	9	1	10	10
−8	+1	+9	−1	−9

59. Practice sheet for addition and subtraction of numbers from 6 through 10.

enjoy playing a greater variety of games. An adaptation of parchesi may be made by the children. A story they have enjoyed may be the basis of the game. A route is marked on a large card along which the children draw or color episodes from the story. They may mark the route into sections and make a spinner on a card that is numbered for scoring. The numbers on the card must be within the child's computational ability. One spinner might have the numbers 1, 2, and 3; another, 1 through 5; and another 1 through 10.

Such games teach the children cooperation, honesty, and consideration for others; give experience in the use of number; and provide pleasant recreation.

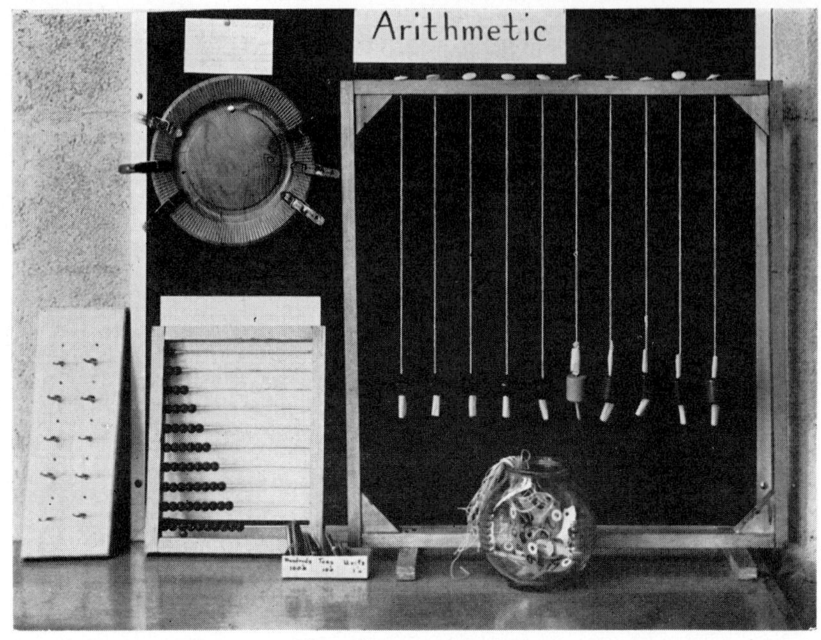

60. Counting devices.

Teaching the Numbers from 6 Through 10. The teacher must take plenty of time to present the next group of numbers. The larger values will require more time for the memory and comprehension processes to function. The importance of the teacher's taking the work slowly cannot be overemphasized. Even though she has given meticulous presentations for the numbers 1 through 5, she must continue to do so for every item that is presented, *over-teaching,* if possible.

Large, tangible objects which the child can handle over and over should be used for counting. At first regular shaped objects, all of the same color, should be used so there will be no distraction. The teacher should check over the materials she has for counting and try to add some new ones for variety, using new colors to change the appearance of the old spools, sticks, and blocks.

She should begin using the abacus, now that the number concepts to five have been established. Small plastic toys are excellent to use for counters and to give variety to games and oral problems.

2 2 1 4 3
+2 +1 +1 +1 +1

2 2 1 3 4 5
-2 -1 -1 -1 -1 -1

2 3 2 4 1 5
-1 -1 -2 -1 -1 -1

1 2 2 3 1 4 3 1
+1 +1 +2 +2 +2 +1 +1 +3

1 2 1 1 3 1 4
+0 +3 +1 +2 +2 +4 +0

61. Practice sheet—addition and subtraction with answers of 5 or less.

Other devices may be constructed to slow down the pupil in counting by rote, in order to attain comprehension of the value of the number in the series. One such device is a board about ¾ x 6 x 12 inches with 10 screw-eyes lightly turned into the wood. As the child counts, he turns each screw-eye in rotation.

Another device is a mobile abacus for counting. This may be made on a rod or suspended on a frame. Ten large wooden beads are individually strung on cords and hung from the rod or frame. The child grasps a bead and says the name of the number. Then he lets go of the bead and grasps the next one, repeating its number name in the series.

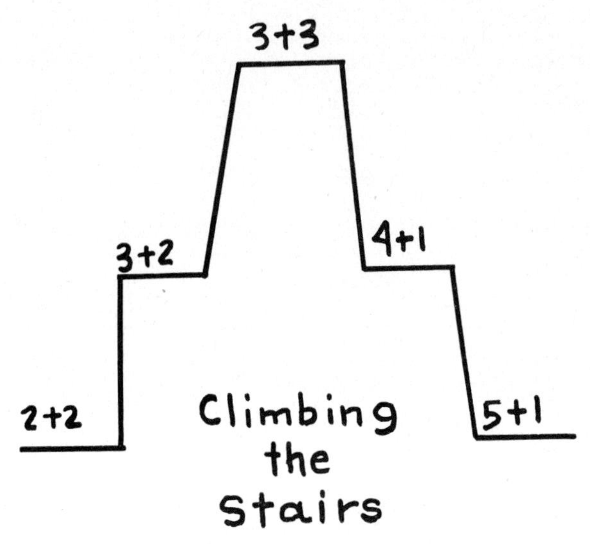

62. A Game—Climbing the Stairs.

A child who has never been able to learn rote counting is thus slowed down by merely picking up each object as he names the corresponding number. As he matures and gains confidence, he is able to count without touching objects.

Presentation of Parallel Facts. At this stage of the presentation of numbers, the addition and subtraction facts for each number starting with six may be taught in the same lessons.

Teaching the Child's Telephone Number. When the child's mental age is 7-0 to 7-6, he should be able to give his address and telephone number. After he has learned them by rote, he can learn to write them. Then he should practice dialing the number in order to learn how to call his home. Later the number of the fire station should be taught for use in an emergency.

Teaching the 45 Basic Addition Combinations. Since ability to count is definitely related to the ability to add, adding and counting are two things that may be taught at the same time. There are 45 basic combinations. It is better to teach the easier 25 combinations whose sums are ten or less first. Then teach the other 20 more difficult combinations and the zero combinations.

The teacher may adapt games to facilitate the retention of the combinations. These should be easy enough for enjoyment by the contestants, yet should be challenging. One such game may be called "Climbing the Stairs."

Climbing the Stairs. The object of the game is to see who can go the highest on the stairs, or who can go up and down without missing a number. If the pupil misses, he is out of that game. If the child does all of the combinations correctly, he gains a point for his team.

Using Computational Skills. The child needs to have experiences with real situations to be able to solve problems. The children's own activities may be utilized for problem material. The children must be helped to visualize the situation or to act it out so that they will understand the situation and be able to arrive at a solution.

Action Problems. The teacher should compose for the children problems in which their names and activities are mentioned. These problems should be presented orally by the teacher. They should be simple in construction and easy to solve. The teacher is speaking.

1. Bob, please get 5 books from the table.
   Thank you, Bob. Now give 3 of the books to Sue.
   How many books do you have left?
2. Tom, please get 7 crayons from the box on my desk.
   Give 4 of the crayons to Sherry.
   How many crayons do you have left?
3. Mary, please give 4 blocks to Sue and 3 blocks to Bob.
   Who has more blocks, Sue or Bob?
   How many more blocks?

Teaching About Zero as a Place Holder. The abacus should be frequently used in teaching the position of zero as a place holder and in teaching the meaning of units, tens, and hundreds. It shows the regularity of the numerical system. The beads, manipulated on the wires, make it easy for the pupils to count off any given number and see what the number means.

Teaching Counting by Twos. When a child is able to count by rote and knows the meaning of *two*, he is ready to learn about pairs of things. As his ability progresses to 4, 6, 8, or 10, he should learn to count the even numbers and the odd numbers. The children like to play games or chant rhymes that help make the idea of pairs meaningful. Objects used in counting, such as disks, beads, buttons, blocks, toys or felt circles, should be utilized in practicing counting the *even* and the *odd* numbers.

Teaching Counting by Fives. To introduce counting by fives, the teacher may tell the children the old story of the shepherd who kept track of his flock with a pile of pebbles. As each sheep passed out of the fold, the shepherd put a pebble in his pocket. The shepherd carried the pebbles about with him all day as he guarded the sheep.

At night as the sheep went back into the pen, he took out a pebble for each sheep. He knew the right number of sheep were in the pen when there were no more pebbles. If the shepherd had one pebble left, he knew a sheep was lost. The children like to play the same game with old pocket books and pebbles. They may take turns counting one another as they march around the room.

Later the teacher may continue the story by showing how the shepherd often had a very heavy pouch of pebbles to carry, until he finally thought of tallying the sheep by five as they went in and out of the fold. A child may hold the pouch and put the fifth pebble in it for every fifth child in the room. The children will see how much easier it is to carry the pouch with fewer pebbles in it.

During this demonstration the teacher should introduce the ordinal *fifth* parallel with teaching the children to count by fives. As the children march she may reverse the procedure by having the keeper of the pouch take a pebble out of it for every five children that pass by him. This teaching should be reinforced by using objects and by counting by fives on the abacus.

Teaching Counting by Tens. After the value of zero as a place holder has been reviewed, the teacher may use objects to demonstrate counting by tens. The game of the shepherd boy may also be continued. Learning the names of the tens and counting by tens help to place the decades. This training should be done regularly in oral and written practice.

Presenting the Teens. Before presenting the teens, the teacher should give the class a thorough review of the numbers 1 through 10, and of zero as a place holder. The children must be helped to see that the numbers after the 9 are two-place numbers. They must understand that 11 is not just two ones side by side, but that 11 is made up of a 10 and a 1. Objects, counters and the abacus should be used to make the child comprehend the real meaning of 11. The child should handle these materials, as the kinesthetic and tactile senses help reinforce the memory.

Each separate *teen* should be taught in this manner. Comprehending the meaning of the teens is one of the most difficult feats the mentally retarded child must make in beginning numbers. If this concept is not established, the rest of the number system will remain a puzzle to him.

Understanding the Tens to One Hundred. Objects should be available for showing the numbers from 1 through 100. The abacus may be used, as it is easily handled. However, the actual handling and counting of objects provide better understanding in the beginning. The children may have a box of counting sticks and some rubber bands to make up bundles of ten sticks until they have ten bundles. As each one counts, he will become aware of the value of ten and of the number of tens it takes to make one hundred.

The teacher must be alert to devise different ways to present these concepts. One particularly slow child was unable to realize the meaning of the tens and hundreds until he was taken out of doors and allowed to collect pebbles by tens and put them in squares drawn on the ground with a stick. Tom drew ten squares and put ten pebbles in each square. This, for some unknown reason, was more understandable to him than putting 10 beans on top of ten squares drawn with chalk on the classroom floor.

The other children in the room became so intrigued with Tom's game that they played it too. The school yard was decorated for a long time with little mounds of pebbles arranged in tens. Tom's game makes an excellent experience for learning the values of hundreds to thousands, or for counting by 2's, 3's, or 5's.

During inclement weather a section of the floor in the classroom may be lined off and grains of corn used for counters. Large sheets of newsprint may be marked off into squares for counting by tens or hundreds. When ten such sheets are used, the children can readily see the hundreds that make the thousands.

Understanding for all will not come in one lesson or even in a dozen demonstrations; the teacher must be patient and repeat the lesson with new variations.

A game of fishing for numbers may be called "The Fish Bowl Game." This game is excellent for a review of recognizing the numbers. The directions for the game are simple.

The teacher may cut small fish from orange construction paper, tie a string through the head of the fish, put a number on each fish, and put the fish into a real fish bowl. The children take turns choosing a string to pull out a fish from the bowl. Each child who can say the number on the fish correctly keeps the fish for a score of 1. If he cannot say the number, he must put the fish back into the bowl.

Continuing Practice in Grouping. The children need continued practice in grouping and in quick recognition of quantities in groups. They will enjoy a card game that teaches *more, less, fewer,* and *greater.*

The teacher constructs the cards of lightweight cardboard about 3 x 6 inches in size on which are placed dots ranging from 1 through 10. The pupils play the game by comparing the groups of dots with a set the teacher presents to gain an understanding of the above terms.

The children may take turns in playing, as in any card game. One card is placed face up on the table; the rest are placed face down. Each child selects a card. If the face card has four dots, the first child to play compares his card with it. If his card has seven dots, he should say, "My card has more dots than four." He then keeps the card, which counts one point for him. He draws another card and the next child plays.

If this next child has a card with less dots than four, but calls them more than four, he puts the card on the bottom of the pile of cards in the center of the table, and draws another card.

The game should also be played using the terms *fewer* and *greater.* As the children's knowledge of number improves, more cards may be added until they have two complete sets of cards

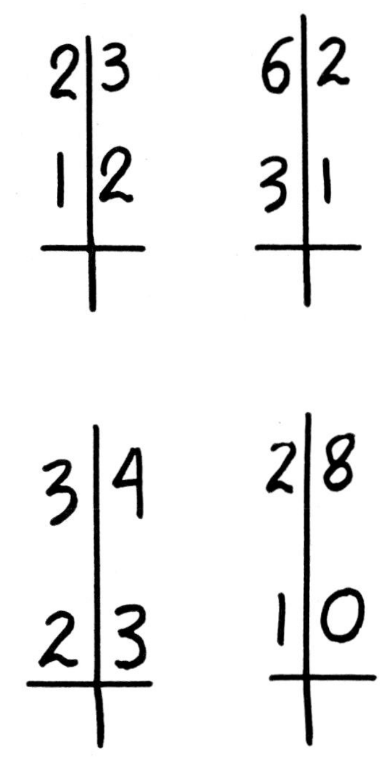

63. Introducing two-place addition.

from which to choose. The scoring may be made more difficult as the pupils' ability improves.

Presenting Two-Place Addition. The child whose mental age is around 8-0 may be ready for addition with two-place numbers, but with no carrying. In constructing examples, put the larger number at the top of the column and instruct the child to add down. He should be able to do partial counting. At first draw lines between the numbers in the units and tens column. The child can see the familiar examples he has been working with and will have confidence in his ability to find the sum.

After he has worked many pages of examples with this device, the guide lines should be left off the examples on part of the page and finally left off entirely. When the child has confidence in the above procedure, the teacher should then present subtraction in the same manner with two-place numbers, but with no borrowing.

Teaching About Borrowing and Carrying. The child must have a good understanding of the tens and the units values before the teacher starts to present carrying and borrowing. Here again it is more satisfactory to begin with addition and to teach carrying.

Pennies and dimes are excellent materials to use to teach the meaning of this process. The abacus is another good device for explaining units, tens, and hundreds. The teacher may use blocks, peg boards, or spool boards with the counters arranged in rows of tens to show how to carry in addition examples. After carrying in addition has been mastered, these same materials may be used to demonstrate borrowing in subtraction examples.

Only two addends should be used in two-place numbers in addition until after subtraction has been mastered for two-place numbers with borrowing. Then hundreds may be taught for addition and later for subtraction. The teacher should prepare simple examples at first, being sure that zero is included and is understood.

The three-place examples should have no borrowing or carrying until the children are secure in using the larger numbers. The teacher will prepare examples beginning with the borrowing or carrying in the tens only. After they have become accustomed to this type of example, she presents the three-place examples with no carrying or borrowing in the tens but with carrying or borrowing in the hundreds. When they have mastered this process, the teacher presents three-place examples with borrowing and carrying in the units, tens, and hundreds.

Reading Larger Numbers. Extensive practice should be given in reading numbers from 1 through 1,000. The teacher should drill the children on the place values of numbers in the position of units, tens, hundreds, and thousands. She should not confuse the children by preparing drills in which the order of the place numbers has been scrambled, but should use the numbers in a manner that corresponds to reality in buying and selling.

Introducing Multiplication. Multiplication may be presented when the child has a mental age of about 8-6 to 9-0 years. The teacher may introduce multiplication first through pairs of objects, then by doubles of numbers, and by the use of addition combinations of doubles. These facts will be familiar to the children from other drills and games. The two's are usually quickly learned.

Relationship of Numbers

$0+6=6$ $6-0=6$

$1+5=6$ $2\times3=6$

$7-1=6$

$2+4=6$

$3\times2=6$

$3+3=6$

$8-2=6$

$1\times6=6$

$4+2=6$

$9-3=6$

$5+1=6$ $6\times1=6$

$10-4=6$

$6+0=6$

$12\div2=6$

64. Presenting the relationship of numbers.

As understanding develops, the children are ready for a few new multiplication facts. These should be introduced gradually with ample demonstrations by the teacher and many class activities by the pupils. To insure understanding and retention will take many years, since other concepts in numbers are being developed at the same time.

When the child has become confident of his ability to multiply with one-place numbers, he is ready to be advanced to two- and three-place numbers with one multiplier and no carrying of tens and shown the use of zero in the units and tens place only after confidence has been gained in the process without carrying.

Introducing Division. Simple division with even numbers may be taught after comprehension and retention in the multiplication of simple numbers have been established. The division facts may be taught by using objects and by intensive drill. Division understanding progresses more slowly than multiplication. Most educable mentally retarded will gain little proficiency in division.

Presenting the Relationship of Numbers. After the child has some experience with addition, subtraction, multiplication and division, a series of examples may be used to produce the same answers. This type of exercise will have meaning only for the children with the highest mental age in the group. The teacher should prepare the examples and go over them first with the children; then let the children ask questions about the examples.

If the children are unable to think of questions to ask regarding the relationship of numbers, the teacher may demonstrate the examples again. Then she may distribute examples without the answers for the children to solve. She should not be discouraged if she secures litle progress in establishing this concept, because the educable mentally retarded will be able to work the simple problems that fulfill their needs without a complete understanding of the relationships of numbers.

OTHER TOPICS

At regular intervals short units on other topics are taught. These should include money values, shapes, linear measurement, weights, dry and liquid measures, fractional parts, time, the calendar, the clock, the days of the week, the months of the year, the holidays, and the Roman numerals.

Presenting Money Values. Begin with real money to teach a child to make change. He will then have a correct image of the coins about which he is studying. After the correct concept has been established, use play money. Work with the child independently until he learns a few values. Then let him work in group activities with children who are on about the same level of ability in handling money.

Teach the values of the one cent and the nickel concurrently with the study of the values of the numbers through five. When the child has learned the numbers from 6 through 10, teach him the value of the dime. Keep reviewing the cents and the nickel so that he will not forget them. *Go slowly.*

Present the larger values of money as the child matures and attains a readiness for them. Do not hurry this presentation, which should be started only after the concept of the corresponding number has been established. For example, present the quarter, 25c in change, and making change for a quarter only after the concept of the number 25 has been established.

When the child understands the number system up to 100, he is ready to learn the value of the dollar, the meaning of the decimal sign, the dollar sign, reading and writing the values of money in dollars and cents, and to solve practical problems about money.

The basic values are learned through individual instruction. The child will become proficient in recognizing money values and in making change through units of work about the grocery store, the post office, and other school activities.

The children should have practice in reading money values. This may be accomplished by writing amounts on the chalkboard, by allowing the class to practice reading them, and by pronouncing amounts to the children for them to write.

By the time the educable mentally retarded child is ready to leave the intermediate department he should be able to use money up to ten dollars in buying and selling at the school play store. Trading at the play store should be done with play money to avoid complications resulting from too much temptatioin.

Teach money values once or twice a week consistently so that the children will be competent and confident in handling money. Every teacher should encourage the children and be persistent in following through regularly in this process, because it is one of the valuable skills the child should attain for self-sufficiency

Presenting Shapes. Shapes should be incidentally taught to children from an early age at home. These are usually presented informally to the group of the primary age mentally retarded. Systematic instruction is started when the children arrive in the intermediate age group. Teach in this order the circle, square, triangle, rectangle, or oblong by using the following: stencils; forms to trace around; emery board cut-outs; forms drawn on the chalkboard or on paper to be colored solidly within the lines.

Show the pupils the circle, square, triangle, and rectangle forms that are to be found in the classroom. Ask the children to think of these forms and tell where they have been seen in other places. The entire presentation should not be hurried, but should cover about a two- to three-year period.

The older retarded group should learn about the cube, cylinder, and sphere. These forms are used in everyday living in such items as food containers, balls, utensils, or as parts of our homes.

Presenting Linear Measurement. The educable mentally retarded have great difficulty in recognizing distance. Since the idea of any linear measurement is vague and incomprehensible to them, things are usually referred to as far away, close, not very big, big, tall, not very tall. These concepts should be used as a basis for enlarging and extending the values of measurements.

The child becomes aware of the value of measurement and of the unit of the inch through being measured in the health clinic. When he demonstrates an interest in measurement, show him how to measure an inch and how to make a ruler one inch long. Make the ruler from a strip of inch-squared paper, which the pupil cuts into strips one-inch long. Linear measurement should be concurrently taught with learning the number system and with rote counting.

As the use of number increases, so will the concept of measurement. The pupil will learn the term *foot ruler* before he learns 12 inches. He can begin to measure in inches as soon as he learns to count one and one. This child must be shown the procedure to use in measuring a line. The teacher should talk to the child about the ruler and explain its use. She should show the child how to lay the ruler on the paper; how to hold the ruler to keep it from wiggling; how to make a dot at the exact end of the ruler and at the one-inch line; how to carefully draw between the dots without moving the ruler.

As each child gains mastery of drawing the one-inch line, the group may work together. The teacher may make a game of giving the directions in a brief rhythmic tone as she moves among the children and helps them to secure competency.

At a mental age of 7-0 to 7-6 years, the children may start to measure many things such as books, pencils, crayons, and desks. They may draw lines of stated length, or measure lines drawn on the chalkboard.

At the mental age of 7-6 to 8-0 years, the child may be expected to know the use of the foot ruler and the number of inches in a foot. He is now ready to be taught the use of the yardstick. He should learn that three feet make a yard, that 36 inches also make one yard, and that the yardstick is used to measure things that are larger than books and desks. He may measure the *length* of the room, the *width* of the hall, and learn to use those terms.

When the child attains a mental age of 8-6 or better, he should be taught about longer distances. To present the idea of a mile, instruct him to walk around the block three times, which is approximately one mile, according to the usual city block.

Discuss the length of time required to go various distances, as to the post office, to the grocery store, to school, to another city. Talk about how the trip was made, whether by car, by train, by plane, or by walking. The child should be made aware of measurement in everyday living.

Presenting Weights and Measures. Until the educable mentally retarded child has a mental age of 7-6 to 8-0 years, he should not be expected to understand weights or measures. This, of course, depends upon his environment and experience.

Teach the *pound* first, as the child usually has some experience with a pound of coffee or a pound of butter. Give him some experience in handling weights of a pound, a half-pound, more than a pound, and less than a pound.

Small desk scales may be used to demonstrate how the pointer moves to indicate the various weights of articles. Stress the value of the pound through class activity such as the grocery store, the post office, or the market. Also, introduce through study of the post office or drug store the smaller unit of weight, the ounce.

Instruct the child with a mental age of 8-0 to 8-6 years about liquid measures, limiting the basic units of measure to a cup, a quart, a pint, and a gallon. Teach the dry measures of the quart, pint, and bushel at this time.

Collective units should also be introduced at this mental age. The terms pair, dozen and half-dozen should be taught through the use of gloves, shoes, shoe strings, and egg cartons.

Children with a mental age of 9-0 to 10-0 should be able to acquire a good working knowledge of the basic values in measurement.

Presenting Fractional Parts. The child may know the term one-half when he starts to school, but still not have the concept that a half is one of two equal parts of a thing. At a mental age of 7-0 years, he is ready to be taught the meaning of the term.

There are commercial items available for teaching fractional parts. One item of value is a wooden fruit plate with three wooden fruits divided into fractional parts for demonstration purposes. Flannel boards with fuzzy circles and squares may be purchased or constructed by the teacher. All of these materials add interest and variety to the lessons on fractions.

Presenting One-Half. The teacher must use ingenuity in making games to present the idea of a fractional part. Children like to use things they can handle or even eat in class. Apples that are cut to show halves may be eaten at the close of the lesson. Small candy rolls may be used similarly by cutting some of them into halves and some into uneven parts. The children may choose matching halves. They may measure the piece chosen against a marker. If the piece chosen is a half, the child may keep the piece of candy.

Matching of halves may be done with sticks, straws, or other

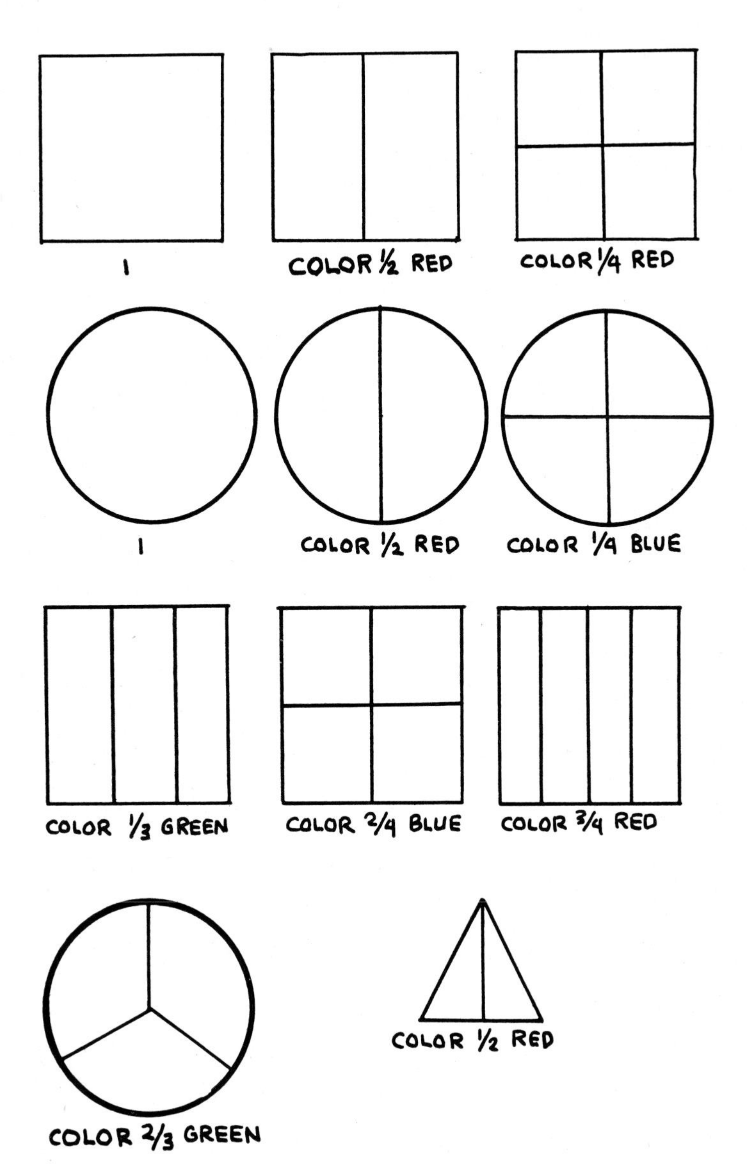

65. A. Presenting shapes and fractional parts.

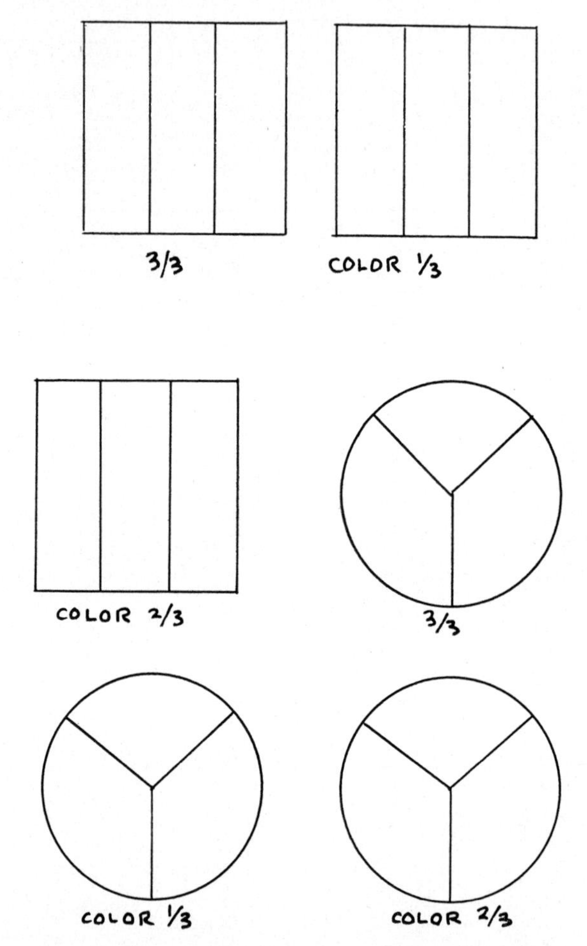

THIS IS A SAMPLE OF ONE TYPE OF WORK SHEET USED IN TEACHING FRACTIONAL PARTS.

66. B. Presenting shapes and fractional parts.

Addition of Fractions

$\frac{1}{2}+\frac{1}{2}=$ $\quad\frac{2}{4}+\frac{1}{4}=$ $\quad\frac{1}{4}+\frac{2}{4}+\frac{1}{4}=$

$\frac{1}{4}+\frac{1}{4}=$ $\quad\frac{2}{4}+\frac{2}{4}=$ $\quad\frac{1}{4}+\frac{3}{4}=$

$\frac{1}{4}+\frac{1}{4}+\frac{1}{4}=$

$\frac{3}{4}+\frac{1}{4}=$ $\quad\frac{1}{3}+\frac{1}{3}=$

$\frac{1}{4}+\frac{1}{4}+\frac{1}{4}+\frac{1}{4}=$

$\frac{2}{3}+\frac{1}{3}=$ $\quad\frac{1}{3}+\frac{2}{3}=$

67. Practice sheet for addition of fractions.

things of interest to the children. The ease of dividing accurately into the parts should be considered when selecting articles for demonstration. These lessons continue throughout the year at regular intervals, so that there is opportunity for review, and so that comprehension and retention will be maintained.

In addition to the above use of three-dimensional materials the teacher should also use forms cut from colored paper. This gives practice in following directions, in developing eye and hand coordination, and in extending the children's comprehension of the concept of one-half to include surface measurements.

A sample lesson is given which demonstrates the method of presenting this concept. The procedure illustrates the detailed explanation and assistance which is necessary for the children's comprehension of simple directions.

Teacher: See this piece of red paper. What shape is this piece of red paper? Yes, it is round, it is a circle. We will call it a red circle. We are going to cut this red circle into two parts. We want each part to be the same size. We want the parts to be *equal. Equal* means the same size, or the same amount.

Each of you may pick up the red circle that is on your desk. Fold the paper together like this. (The teacher holds the red circle in both hands and folds the edges together.)

Be sure the edges are even. (She goes about among the children showing them what is meant by *edges* and *fold.*)

Hold the red paper tightly. Now, with thumb and finger of one hand, crease the red paper down the fold, like this. (The teacher goes from desk to desk, encouraging, helping, showing what is meant by a *crease,* and praising each child.)

Now, take the scissors and cut along the fold. (Some children will need help in cutting a straight line along the crease in the red paper.)

Put the pieces of paper on the desk. Put them side by side. How many pieces do you have? Into how many pieces did you cut the whole red circle? (Give the children time to look and to reply.)

Impress upon the children that a thing is only cut into halves when the cut pieces are of equal size. The children may paste the halves of the red circles into their arithmetic notebooks. The teacher should help them to write ½ under each part of the red circle.

Repeat this procedure many times using forms cut from colored paper and three-dimensional forms. Keep the directions simple. Do not confuse the children by naming the parts of the fraction—the denominator and numerator. Instead they may repeat, "The bottom number of the fraction tells into how many parts anything has been divided. The top number of the fraction shows how many of the parts were taken or were kept."

When combining ½ and ½, show the children that 1 and 1 make 2, and then that when 2 is over 2, it shows 2 equal parts or the whole apple or thing. Teach the word *halves* orally first for auditory recognition of the word; then much later present it for visual recognition.

The teacher should instruct the children to count the parts of the apple, to write the number 2, to draw a line *under* the 2, to count into how many parts the apple was cut, and to write down the number 2 *under* the line. She should say, "Now you have two halves." If the children do not appear to understand, she must repeat and reinforce the teaching; give further demonstrations; repeat the key questions and give the answers until the children show comprehension. Another process or step should not be started until this one is thoroughly understood.

Separating Groups into Fractions. The flannel board is a good device to use in demonstrating how to divided a group of things into fractions. The teacher should place two disks of contrasting color on the flannel board. Black disks on a white flannel board are stimulating to the children. The teacher talks to the children.

Teacher: How many black spots do you see?

Pupils: Two black spots.

Teacher: Tom, you may take away one of the black spots. You have taken away one-half of the black spots. Tom, how many black spots make one-half of two black spots?

Repeat this procedure many times, using other materials until the children understand without prompting that 2 is one-half of 4 is similar. It may be further dramatized by using four children each with a real apple. The teacher separates the children into two groups. Each group keeps half of the apples.

Presenting One-Fourth. The fractional part of one-fourth may be shown to the child when he has attained the mental age of 7-6 or better. The same techniques should be used as were outlined for teaching the concept one-half. Since one-fourth is more difficult to present than one-half, do not hurry, but continue through every step of the explanation to secure comprehension for this new concept.

Continue to drill with circles, squares, and fruits cut from paper. Use the flannel board and felt disks to demonstrate the fractional part of a group. Help the child to realize that four-fourths make a whole apple, or *one* of anything.

Presenting One-Third. When the child has a mental age of 8-0 years or better, he is ready for the idea of thirds. Introduce in the same manner as one-half. After working for some time with ⅓, review ½ and ¼. Use small juice glasses marked with the fractional parts of ½, ¼, and ⅓ to test the child's knowledge of parts and wholes. Prepare stencils or make worksheets for the children to color the fractional part as named.

There should be practice on writing and naming the fractional parts, such as ½, ¼, and ⅓. As understanding develops, combine the fractional parts with similar denominators. A child with a mental age of 9-0 years will be able to add simple fractions with no sum greater than the whole, or *one*.

Presenting Time, the Calendar, and the Clock. Teaching the concept of time, as in other basic skills, requires a certain degree of maturity before understanding may be expected. The child needs to be conscious of time from the first day of school. Punctuality is a requirement for holding any position or job. The educable mentally retarded are seldom aware of the passage of time unless it is emphasized for them. This must be done with study and drill during their formative years.

The concepts about time that one may expect the educable mentally retarded to find useful are listed in this chapter in the Progress Chart with the approximate mental age at which the child should be able to comprehend and retain the material. The presentation of the material should be extended through a teaching period of about three years. At all mental ages children vary in their interests and ability to retain.

They may advance rapidly in one step of learning through the use of certain materials; again they may reach a plateau where more readiness must be given. The readiness must continue until they reach a stage of maturity where the next step of the learning process may be understood and absorbed. The teacher must be alert for these plateaus of learning, and for the period of readiness which usually follows after adequate preparation.

Presenting the Concept of Time. There are many devices available commercially for teaching time. However, devices may also be constructed in the classroom or shop. A large clock face may be made from plywood or heavy cardboard, with large numerals painted on the face. The hour and minute hands should be attached so that they turn to show the time.

A child who can tell time may be appointed as the clock monitor. He will keep the clock set for the next activity throughout the day. Each child should have an opportunity to be clock monitor.

A real clock should also be used for experience in telling time. An old clock serves the purpose of showing how the hands turn. The time values should be presented as outlined in the schedule as the child shows readiness. After explaining the meaning of the hours, half-hour, minutes, and quarter hour values, introduce the child to telling time by minutes.

The child should be shown the correct way to write time and how to read it. This can be done when the child can count by 5's to 55. He should be shown how to first write the hour, then the colon, and finally the minutes, as 2:35.

Prepare sheets for practice by stamping circles on ditto carbon sheets. The teacher should make sets of clock faces similar to the illustrations for each phase of presenting time. For the child who can count to five, she should use only those numerals he recognizes by sight, or from 1 through 5. The child should have sets of clock faces made for each number as he learns to recognize it and can count to it by rote.

68. Worksheet–sample clock faces for teaching the hour and half-hour.

69. Worksheet–sample clock faces for teaching the quarter-hour.

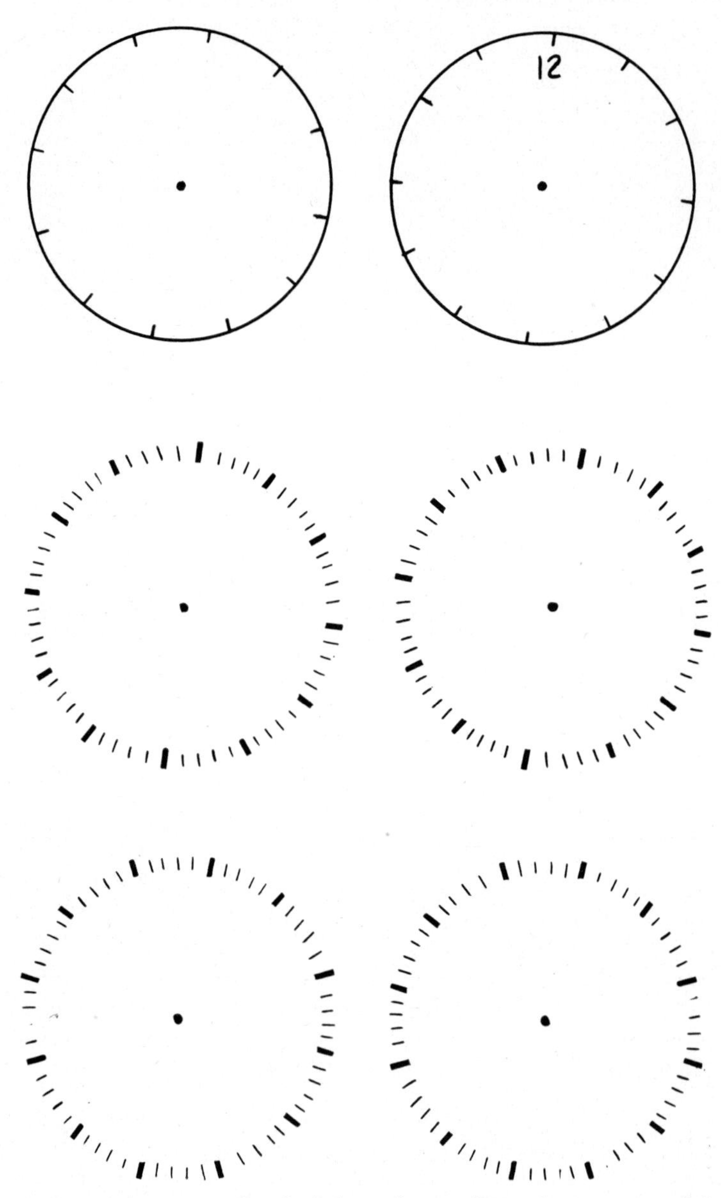

70. Worksheet—sample clock faces for teaching the minute and five minute intervals of time.

Sun.	Mon.	Tues.	Wed.	Thurs.	Fri.	Sat.

71. Calendar Form—for teaching months, weeks, and days.

The teacher should make up the same kind of sets of clock faces to show the half-hour through the use of the numbers 6 and 12. Then she should add other numbers to show the hour hand at all positions.

The teacher should stress the position of the hands of the clock in telling time by the quarter-hour. The numbers on the clock face should be 12, 3, 6, and 9 for the first presentation. Then other numbers are added to show the hours, but the accent is on the quarter after the hour or the quarter before the hour. Counting by five may be started to establish the concept of fifteen minutes until, or fifteen minutes after the hour.

The child should have practice in drawing the hands on the clock faces to indicate the time as shown below the clock on a worksheet.

The teacher should prepare circles with heavy lines of color to mark the five-minute intervals instead of the numbers. The children learn to count from the top mark by fives. Then the number 12 is placed at the top of the clock face under the colored mark. The child continues the practice of counting by fives until this can be done correctly.

The next step is to make the minute intervals with a different color, diminishing the size of the markings as the child becomes secure in counting by fives and by ones to 60. Then use one color on all of the minute and hour marks on the clock face and finally put on all of the numbers. Drill should be continued for accuracy in telling time.

Presenting the Days of the Week. The educable mentally retarded need to learn the names of the days of the week, and to know them in sequence. Awareness of the days of the week and of the months of the year may be taught by using a mimeographed calendar form and a large wall calendar.

A calendar should be started the first day of school. The first period of the day is the best time for this activity. The teacher must be consistent in presenting this activity. She may ask the children for the name of the month, the day, the date, and the season of the year, which someone in the group will usually know. If no one does, the teacher will supply the information. After she has written the day of the week and the date, she will read it to the class. Then the children will read the information in unison.

The teacher should talk about the calendar, pointing out the day, the name of the month, and the date. Since the names of the days on most calendars are abbreviated, the children should be taught to recognize them, as well as the entire name.

The children may keep a record of the weather on the small mimeographed calendar forms. They may use familiar symbols, such as a circle with rays for the sun, an umbrella for rain, and irregular forms for clouds. Keeping this record will make the children aware of many things concerning the weather which they have never noticed previously.

Along with the calendar exercises, discussions may be held concerning morning, afternoon, and dismissal time. The children become aware that noon is the time when morning ends and afternoon begins. Much later the teacher introduces evening, midnight, and then the letters that indicate morning and afternoon, A.M., and P.M.

Through imitation and repetition the children gradually learn to write time correctly. As the seasons change and the days become longer or shorter, the children become aware that the sun is shining when they get up in the morning, or that the sun does not shine until long after they have had breakfast. Even though they may not fully understand why this fact is true, they should be aware of the changes. They should also be made aware of the difference in the length of days and nights and of the seasons in other parts of the world than their home land.

A social studies unit is of value in teaching the differences in climate in the countries of the world. The educable mentally retarded are usually aware of other countries through the radio, television, pictures in newspapers, and through their contact with relatives in the armed services. Many teachers and visitors from other countries come to the schools almost daily to find out how the children are instructed in this country. They often contribute interesting information that helps the children realize something of the size of the world, and the variety of climatic conditions of the world.

Presenting Roman Numerals. The teacher should tell the children about Roman numerals and explain and demonstrate the system from 1 through 20. The children will see these numbers on some clock faces and at the beginning of chapters in some books; therefore, they should be made aware of the meaning of the symbols. They may be interested to know the meaning of the I, V, X, and some of the combinations. There is no need to drill on learning the combinations; that is an unimportant item for the mentally retarded.

SUMMARY

The teacher of the educable mentally retarded has a great responsibility before her that will demand patience, persistence endurance, love, and humility. She must realize that developing understanding within the damaged or malformed brain of these children requires gearing her activities and work plans for them to a slow repetitive pattern.

She should not allow the children's superficial ability to confuse her objectives. She must realize that true understanding is needed to make arithmetic useful, and that every small detail must be explained and demonstrated to secure the necessary comprehension. All of these skills and abilities should be taught with one purpose in mind—to produce happy, useful citizens.

BIBLIOGRAPHY

1. Abel, Theodora M., and Kinder, Elaine: *The Subnormal Adolescent Girl.* New York, Columbia University Press, 1942.

2. Abraham, Willard: *A Guide for the Study of Exceptional Children.* Boston, Porter Sargent, Publishers, 1955.

3. Abraham, Willard: *Barbara: A Prologue.* New York, Rinehart and Company, Incorporated, 1958.

4. Allen, Amy A.: *Let Us Teach Slow Learning Children.* Columbus, Ohio, State Department of Education, 1950.

5. Anderson, V. E.: *Principles and Procedure of Curriculum Improvement.* New York, Ronald Press, 1956.

6. Arnholter, Ethelwyne: Social Drama for Retarded Adolescents, *Exceptional Children, 21:*132-134, January 1955.

7. Arnold, Ruth Gifford: Speech Rehabilitation for the Mentally Retarded, *Exceptional Children, 22:*50-52, November 1955.

8. Association for Supervision and Curriculum Development. *The Three R's in the Elementary School.* Washington, D. C., National Education Association, 1952.

9. Atwater, M. M.: *Byways in Handweaving.* New York, Macmillan Company, 1954.

10. Axline, Virginia: *Play Therapy.* New York, Houghton Mifflin Company, 1947.

11. Baker, Harry J.: *Introduction to Exceptional Children,* rev. ed., New York, Macmillan Company, 1953.

12. Baldwin, Willie Kate: The Educable Mentally Retarded Child in the Regular Grades, *Exceptional Children, 25:*106-108, November 1959.

13. Baskin, J. W.: Vitalizing Experiences for Ungraded Pupils, *Chicago School Journal,* Talcott School, March-April 1952.

14. Bender, Lauretta: *Agression, Hostility, and Anxiety in Children.* Springfield, Illinois, Charles C Thomas, Publisher, 1954.

15. Benoit, Paul E., and Wallace, Robert: A Philosophy of Discipline, *American Journal of Mental Deficiency, 61:* July 1956.
16. Benoit, Paul E.: The Play Problem of Retarded Children, *American Journal of Mental Deficiency, 60:*41, July 1955.
17. Birch, Jack W., and Stevens, Godfrey D.: *Reaching the Mentally Retarded.* Bloomington, Illinois, Public School Publishing Company, 1955.
18. Blatt, Burton: The Physical, Personality, and Academic Status of Children Who are Mentally Retarded Attending Special Classes as Compared with Children Who are Mentally Retarded Attending Regular Classes, *American Journal of Mental Deficiency, 63:*810-818, March 1958.
19. Blough, G. O.: *Making and Using Classroom Science Materials in the Elementary School.* New York, Dryden Press, 1954.
20. Bond, L. G., and Tinker, M.: *Reading Difficulties: Their Diagnosis and Correction.* New York, Appleton-Century-Crofts, 1957.
21. Borreca, Frank, and others: *A Functional Core Vocabulary for Slow Learners.* Reprint from *American Journal of Mental Deficiency.* New York, 1420 Wood Road, Box 62, *58:* October 1953.
22. Buck, Pearl: *The Child Who Never Grew.* New York 1, John Day Company, 9 West 29th Street, 1950.
23. Burt, Cyril L. *The Subnormal Mind,* 3rd. ed. London, Oxford University Press, 1956.
24. Capobianco, R. J., and Cole, Dorothy A.: Social Behavior of Mentally Retarded Children, *American Journal of Mental Deficiency, 64:*638-651, January 1960.
25. Carabo-Cone, Madaline: *How to Help Children Learn Music.* New York, Harper & Brothers, 1955.
26. Carrison, D., and Werner, Heinz: Principles and Methods of Teaching Arithmetic to Mentally Retarded Children, *American Journal of Mental Deficiency, 47:*209-217, January 1943.
27. Catholic University of America: *Workshop on Music Education,* 1953 and 1954. *Workshop on Special Education of the Exceptional Child,* 1954. Washington, D. C., Catholic University of America.
28. Cleary, F. D.: *Individual and Group Guidance Suggestions for Classroom Teachers.* Detroit, Wayne University Press, 1953.

29. Cleigh, M. F.: *The Slow Learner, Some Educational Principles and Policies.* New York, Philosophical Library, 1957.

30. Cole, Lenore: Sources of Audio-Visual Materials for Survey of Job Areas, Buffalo 22: *Exceptional Children Education's Operation Assistance,* State University of New York, College of Teachers, 1958.

31. Cruickshank, W. M.: *Education of Exceptional Children and Youth.* New York, Prentice-Hall, 1958.

32. Cruickshank, W. M.: *Psychology of Exceptional Children and Youth.* Englewood, New Jersey, Prentice-Hall, 1955.

33. Curtis, Ethel L.: Building Toward Academic Readiness in Mentally Deficient Children, *American Journal of Mental Deficiency, 48:*183-187, October 1943.

34. Dale, Edgar: *Audio-Visual Methods in Teaching,* rev. ed. New York, Dryden Press, 1954.

35. D'Amico, V. E.: *Art for the Family.* New York, Simon and Schuster, 1954.

36. Daniels, A. S.: *Adapted Physical Education.* New York, Harper & Brothers, 1954.

37. Dawe, Ann Miller: Trends Toward the Extension of Special Services for the Educable Mentally Handicapped at the Junior School Level, *American Journal of Mental Deficiency, 61:*692-697, April 1957.

38. Deans, Edwina: *Arithmetic Children Use.* Washington, D. C., Association for Childhood Education, 1954.

39. Descoeudres, Alice: *The Education of Mentally Defective Children.* Translated from the Second French Edition by E. F. Ross. New York, D. C. Heath and Company, 1928.

40. D'Evelyn, Katherine E.: *Meeting Children's Emotional Needs.* Englewood Cliffs, N. J., Prentice-Hall, 1957.

41. Devereux, George: *Therapeutic Education.* New York, Harper & Brothers, 1956.

42. DiMichael, Salvatore F.: *Vocational Rehabilitation of the Mentally Retarded.* Washington, D. C., United States Government Printing Office, 1950.

43. Dolch, Edward W.: *Helping the Educationally Handicapped.* Champaign, Illinois, Garrard Press, 1950.

44. Doll, E. A.: *The Measurement of Social Competence.* Minneapolis, Minn., Educational Test Bureau, 1953.

45. Driscoll, Gertrude: *How to Study the Behavior of Children.* New York, Columbia University Press, 1954.

46. Durrell, Donald D.: *Improvement of Basic Reading Abilities.* Yonkerson-Hudson, New York, World Book Company, 1956.

47. Ecob, Katherine G.: *The Retarded Child in the Community.* New York, New York State Society for Mental Health, New York 10, 1955.

48. Education Policies Commission: *Policies for Education in American Democracy.* Washington, D. C., National Education Association, 1946.

49. English, Horace B., and Ava C.: *Comprehensive Dictionary of Psychological and Psychoanalytical Terms.* New York, Longmans, Green and Co., Inc., 1958.

50. Featherstone, W. B.: *Teaching the Slow Learner,* rev. ed., New York, Teachers College, Columbia University, 1951.

51. Fernald, Grace: *Remedial Techniques in Basic School Subjects.* New York, McGraw-Hill Book Company, 1943.

52. Fernald, James C.: *Synonyms, Antonyms, and Prepositions,* rev. ed. by Ed. Staff, New York, Funk and Wagnalls Company, 1947.

53. Fouracre, Maurice H.: Learning Characteristics of Brain Injured Retarded Children, *Exceptional Children, 25:*210-213, January 1958.

54. Frank, John P.: *My Son's Story.* New York, A. A. Knopf, 1951.

55. Freeman, Frank N.: How to Deal With Left-Handedness, *National Education Association, 49:* January 1950.

56. Freeman, Kenneth: *Helping Children Understand Science.* Philadelphia, Winston, 1954.

57. Gaitskill, C. D.: Art Education for Slow Learners. Peoria, Illinois, Charles A. Bennett Company, 1953.

58. Garrison, Ivan K.: A Community Approach to a School Program for Exceptional Children, *Exceptional Children, 19:*313-316, May 1953.

59. Garrison, Karl C.: *The Psychology of Exceptional Children.* New York, Ronald Press, 1950.

60. Garton, Malinda Dean.: A Study of Play Therapy: Communication, T-V and Mike, *American Childhood Magazine, 41:*10-12, September 1955.

61. ———: A Thanksgiving Activity, *American Childhood Magazine, 42:*24-26, November 1956.
62. ———: Butterflies, *American Childhood Magazine, 40:*21, May 1955.
63. ———: Children of the Philippines, *American Childhood Magazine, 41:*11-13, June 1956.
64. ———: Children's Pictured Tensions, *American Childhood Magazine, 43:*26-28, December 1957.
65. ———: Emotional Release Through Clay Modeling, Part I, Introduction and Physiological Factors, *American Childhood Magazine, 40:*16-18, December 1954.
66. ———: Emotional Release Through Clay Modeling, Part II, Psychological Factors, *American Childhood Magazine, 40:*16-18, January 1955.
67. ———: Emotional Release Through Clay Modeling, Part III, Environmental Factors, *American Childhood Magazine, 40:*11-13, February 1955.
68. ———: Emotional Release Through Creative Painting for the Mentally Retarded, *American Childhood Magazine, 37:*10-12, April 1952.
69.———: Field Trips Require Careful Plans, *The Instructor, 64:*42, April 1955.
70. ———: Health Instruction for the Slow Learner, *American Childhood Magazine, 43:*16-18, September 1957.
71. ———: Introducing the Slow Learner to Spring, *American Childhood Magazine, 42:*8-11, April 1957.
72. ———: Make a Scrap Book, *Highlights for Children, 10:*40, May 1955.
73. ———: Making Friends, *American Childhood Magazine, 42:*4-6, March 1957.
74. ———: Making Reed Table Mats, *The Instructor, 69:*22, February 1958.
75. ———: Nature Study with Creative Activities, *American Childhood Magazine, 41:*28-29, November 1955.
76. ———: Our Flag, *American Childhood Magazine, 42:*10-11, February 1957.
77. ———: Our National Anthem, *American Childhood Magazine, 42:*4-6, January 1957.

78. ———: Rain Made to Order at School, *The Instructor, 65:*34, September 1955.

79. ———: School Safety, *American Childhood Magazine, 42:*24-26, May 1957.

80. ———: Social and Emotional Growth Through Creative Painting, *American Childhood Magazine, 38:*18-19, June 1953.

81. ———: Teaching the Slow Learner About the Postal Service, *The Instructor, 64:*49, November 1954.

82. ———: The Air Around Us, *The Instructor, 62:*23, February 1953.

83. ———: The Boys' and Girls' Store, *The Instructor, 61:*23, November 1951.

84. ———: The How and Why of Tooth Care, *The Instructor, 63:*38, February 1954.

85. ———: The Mentally Retarded in School, Part II—The Educable Mentally Retarded, *Guide for Exceptional Children,* Bismark, North Dakota. Superintendent of Public Instruction, State of North Dakota, 1956, 80-83.

86. ———: The Penguin, *Grade Teacher, 33:*19, January 1956.

87. ———: Tray Covers and Favors, *American Childhood Magazine, 39:*8, May 1954.

88. ———: Understanding the Mentally Retarded, *American Childhood Magazine, 44:*24-26, April 1958.

89. ———: Vacation Activities at the Beach, *American Childhood Magazine, 40:*16-17, June 1955.

90. ———: Westward Ho, *American Childhood Magazine, 42:*24-26, December 1956.

91. Geri, F. H.: *Illustrated Games and Rhythms for Children in the Primary Grades.* New York, Prentice-Hall, 1955.

92. Goldberg, I. Ignacy: A Survey of the Present Status of Vocational Rehabilitation of the Mentally Retarded Residents in State Supported Institutions, *American Journal of Mental Deficiency, 61:*698-705, April 1957.

93. Goldstein, Herbert, and Seigle, Dorothy: Illinois Guide for Teachers of the Educable Mentally Handicapped, Chicago, Illinois Council for Mentally Retarded Children, 343 South Dearborn Street, Chicago 4, Illinois.

94. Goodenough, Florence: *Exceptional Children.* New York, Appleton-Century-Crofts, 1956.

95. Graham, Ray: *The Educable Mentally Handicapped.* Springfield, Illinois, State Department of Special Education, 1958.

96. Gray, William S.: *The Teaching of Reading and Writing: An International Survey.* Chicago, Unesco and Scott Foresman and Company, 1956.

97. Gunther, John: *Death Be Not Proud: A Memoir.* New York, Harper & Brothers, 1949.

98. Harnett, Mary E.: *Mental Retardation.* Washington, D. C., National Education Association, International Council for Exceptional Children, 1956. A Special Bibliography.

99. Harrison, M. Lucile: *Reading Readiness.* Boston, Houghton Mifflin Company, 1939.

100. Harrison, Sam: Integration of Developmental Language Activities with an Educational Program for Mentally Retarded Children, *American Journal of Mental Deficiency, 63:*967-970, May 1959.

101. Hart, R. G.: *How to Sell Your Handicrafts.* New York, D. McKay Company, 1953.

102. Hartman, Bernard T.: Study of Therapeutic and Functional Values of Hearing Aids for the Mentally Handicapped, *American Journal of Mental Deficiency, 63:*803-809, March 1958.

103. Havighurst, Robert J.: *Human Development and Education.* New York, Longmans, Green and Co., Inc., 1953.

104. Hayes, E. Nelson: *A Directory of Schools for Exceptional Children,* 2nd ed. Boston, Porter Sargent, Publisher, 11 Beacon Street, 1956.

105. Heber, Rick: A Manual on Terminology and Classification in Mental Retardation, A Monograph Supplement to the *American Journal of Mental Deficiency, 64:* September 1959, Albany 10, New York.

106. Heck, Arch O.: *The Education of Exceptional Children.* New York, McGraw-Hill Book Company, 1953.

107. Heilman, H. L.: A Suite for Educable Mentally Retarded Children in the Elementary School, *Exceptional Children, 21:*289-291, May 1955.

108. Hennesey, W. J.: *Things for Boys and Girls to Make.* New York, Harper & Brothers, 1954.

109. Hester, K. B.: *Teaching Every Child to Read.* New York, Harper & Brothers, 1955.

110. Hildreth, Gertrude: *Teaching Spelling.* New York, Henry Holt and Company, 1955.

111. Hill, Arthur S.: *The Forward Look* (The Severely Retarded Child Goes to School). Washington, D. C., Federal Security Agency, Bulletin No. 11, 1952.

112. Hill, Arthur S.: The Status of Mental Retardation Today, *Exceptional Children, 25:*298-299, March 1959.

113. Holme, Geoffrey: *The Children's Art Book.* New York, The Studio Publications, 432 Fourth Avenue, 1954.

114. Hooper, Rodney: *Plastics for the Home Craftsman.* Philadelphia, Lippincott, 1953.

115. Horace Mann-Lincoln Institute Pamphlet. *How to Construct a Sociogram,* 7th printing New York, Bureau of Publications, Teachers College, Columbia University, 1954.

116. Horwich, F. R.: *Have Fun With Your Children.* New York, Prentice-Hall, 1954.

117. Howe, Clifford E.: A Comparison of Motor Skills of Mentally Retarded and Normal Children, *Exceptional Children, 25:* 352-354, April 1959.

118. Hungerford, Richard H.: Education of the Mentally Handicapped in Childhood and Adolescence, *American Journal of Mental Deficiency, 57:* October 1952.

119. Hymes, James L., Jr.: *A Child Development Point of View.* New York, Prentice-Hall, 1955.

120. Hymes, James L., Jr.: *Behavior and Misbehavior.* New York, Prentice-Hall, 1955.

121. Ikeda, Hannah: Adapting the Nursery School for the Mentally Retarded Child, *Exceptional Children, 21:*171-174, February 1955.

122. Illinois Commission for Handicapped Children. *The Educable Mentally Handicapped Child in Illinois,* 4th ed., Chicago 1, Commission for Handicapped Children, 160 North LaSalle Street, 1953.

123. Ingram, Christine P.: *Education of the Slow Learning Child,* 2nd ed., New York, Ronald Press, 1953.

124. Irwin, Ruth Beckey: Oral Language for Slow Learning Children, *American Journal of Mental Deficiency, 64:*32-40, July 1959.

125. Jennings, Helen Hall: *Sociometry in Group Relations.* Washington, D. C., American Council on Education.

126. Jersild, A. T.: *Child Psychology,* 4th ed., New York, Prentice-Hall, 1954.

127. Johnson, D. F.: Art Education for the Educable Mentally Retarded Child, *American Journal of Mental Deficiency, 62:* 442-450, November 1957.

128. Johnson, G. Orville: A Study of Social Position of Mentally Handicapped Children in Regular Grades, *American Journal of Mental Deficiency, 55:*60-89, July 1950.

129. Jordan, Thomas E., and deCharms, Richard: The Achievement Motive in Normal and Mentally Retarded Children, *American Journal of Mental Deficiency, 64:*457-466, November 1959.

130. Kaliski, Lottie: Educational Therapy for Brain-Injured Retarded Children, *American Journal of Mental Deficiency, 57:* July 1953.

131. Kanner, L.: *Child Psychiatry.* Springfield, Illinois, Charles C Thomas, Publisher, 1960.

132. Kelly, Elizabeth: Are We Providing Opportunities for the Older Mentally Retarded? *Exceptional Children, 21:*297-299, May 1955.

133. Kelman, Howard R.: Individualizing the Social Integration of the Mentally Retarded Child, *American Journal of Mental Deficiency, 60:*860-866, April 1956.

134. Kirk, Samuel A.: *Teaching Reading to Slow Learning Children.* Boston, Houghton Mifflin Company, 1940.

135. Kirk, Samuel A., and Johnson, G. Orville: *Educating the Retarded Child.* Boston, Houghton Mifflin Company, 1951.

136. Kirk, Samuel A., Karnes, Merle, and Kirk, Winifred: *You and Your Retarded Child.* New York, Macmillan Company, 1955.

137. Klenke, W. W.: *The Art of Woodburning,* rev. ed., Peoria, Illinois, Bennett, 1954.

138. Kratter, Frederick B.: Color-Blindness in Relation to Normal and Defective Intelligence, *American Journal of Mental Deficiency, 62:*436-441, November 1957.

139. Kraus, Richard: *Play Activities for Boys and Girls.* New York, McGraw-Hill Book Company, 1957.

140. Kuglemass, I. N.: *The Management of Mental Deficiency in Children.* New York. Grune and Stratton, 1954.

141. Lane, Howard, and Beauchamp, Mary: *Human Relations in Teaching.* New York, Prentice-Hall, 1955.

142. Langdon, Grace, and Stout, Irving W.: *Teacher-Parent Interview* New York, Prentice-Hall, 1954.

143. Larom, Mary: *Enameling for Fun and Profit.* New York, David McKay Company, 1954.

144. LaValli, Alice, and Runge, Lillian: Teaching Slow Learners to Read Common Signs, *Exceptional Children, 18:*38-40, November 1951.

145. Lawson, A. R.: *Fun in the Backyard.* New York, David McKay Company, 1954.

146. Leonard, Charles W.: *Why Children Misbehave.* Chicago, Science Research Associates, 1952.

147. Leonard, E. M.: *Counseling with Parents in Early Childhood Eduation.* New York, Macmillan Company, 1954.

148. Levinson, Abraham: *The Mentally Retarded Child: A Guide for Parents.* New York, John Day Company, 1952.

149. Levy, Anna J. V.: *Other People's Children.* New York, Ronald Press, 1956.

150. Lewis, Richard S., Strauss, Alfred A., and Lehtinen, Laura E.: *The Other Child: The Brain-Injured Child.* New York, Grune and Stratton, 1951.

151. Linton, C. D.: *How to Write Reports.* New York, Harper & Brothers, 1954.

152. Lloyd, Frances: *Educating the Sub-Normal Child.* New York, Philosophical Library, 1953.

153. Loewy, Herta: *The Retarded Child: A Guide for Parents and Teachers.* New York, Philosophical Library, 1951.

154. Loewy, Herta: *Training the Backward Child.* New York, Philosophical Library, 1956.

155. Martens, Elise H.: *A Guide to Curriculum Adjustments for Mentally Retarded Children.* Washington, D. C., United States Government Printing Office, 1936.

156. Martin, W. E.: *Reading in Child Development.* New York, Harcourt, Brace and Company, 1954.

157. Martin, William, and Stendler, C. G.: *Child Development.* New York, Harcourt, Brace and Company, 1953.

158. McCartney, Louise D.: Providing Occupational Readiness for Young Mentally Deficient Children of the Non-Familial Type, *American Journal of Mental Deficiency, 62:* January 1958.

159. Michaelis, John U.: *Social Studies for Children in a Democracy.* New York, Prentice-Hall, 1950.

160. Miller, Elsa A.: Cerebral Palsied Children and Their Parents, *Exceptional Children, 24:*300, March 1958.

161. Miller, Josephine V.: *Paper Sculpture and Construction.* Peoria, Illinois, Charles A. Bennett Company, 1957. Excellent suggestions for classroom use.

162. Miller, Robert V.: Social Status and Socioempathic Differences Among Mentally Superior, Mentally Typical, and Mentally Retarded Children, *Exceptional Children, 23:*114-119, December 1956.

163. Morton, Robert Lee: *Teaching Arithmetic in the Elementary School, Volume I, Primary Grades.* New York, Silver Burdett and Company, 1937.

164. National Association for Music Therapy. *Music Therapy.* Chicago, National Association for Music Therapy, 1951.

165. National Council for Social Studies: *Adapting Instruction in the Social Studies to Individual Differences,* 15th Yearbook, 1944; *Skills in Social Studies,* 24th Yearbook, 1953. Washington, D. C., National Education Association.

166. National Society for the Study of Education. *The Education of Exceptional Children,* 49th Yearbook, Part 2. Chicago, University of Chicago Press, 1950.

167. Newkirk, Louis V.: *Integrated Handbook for the Elementary Schools.* Chicago, Silver Burdett and Company, 1940.

168. Newkirk, Louis V., and Zutter, LaVada: *You Can Make It.* New York, Silver Burdett and Company, 1944.

169. New York State University: *Children the Music Makers.* Buffalo, Bureau of Elementary Curriculum Development, 1953.

170. Nugent, Marion A.: *Home Training Manual.* Boston, Department of Mental Health, 15 Ashburton Place, Boston, Massachusetts, 1957. Activities for the child with mental ages from two to six.

171. Osterhaut, Edna Davison: *Teaching the Retarded Child at Home.* Durham, North Carolina, Seaman's Printery, Incorporated, 1950.

172. Oswalt, Edna R.: *Teaching Extremely Retarded Children.* Kent, Ohio, Kent State University Bulletin, January 1950.

173. Parker, Rose E.: Educating the Teachers of Exceptional Children, *Illinois Education, 32:* May 1944.

174. Patton, David H., and Johnson, Eleanor M.: *Spelling and Writing, Teacher's Manual.* Spelling for Word Mastery Series, Columbus 16, Ohio, Charles E. Merrill Books, Incorporated, 1958.

175. Peck, John R.: The Marbridge Plan: A Texas Experiment in Habilitation for Mentally Retarded Youth, Exceptional Children, *24:*346-350, April 1958.

176. Perry, L. D.: *Bird Houses.* Peoria, Illinois, Charles A. Bennett Company, 1955.

177. Phelps, Harold R.: Post School Adjustment of Mentally Retarded Children in Selected Ohio Cities, *Exceptional Children, 23:* 58-62, November 1956.

178. Piaget, Jean: *Origins of Intelligence in Children.* New York, International University Press, 1952.

179. Plekhonov, O. V.: *Art and Social Life.* London, Lawrence and Wishart, 1953.

180. Podolsky, Edward: *The Jealous Child.* New York, Philosophical Library, 1954.

181. Pollock, Morris, and Pollock, Miriam: *New Hope for the Retarded.* Boston, Porter Sargent Publisher, 1953.

182. Puner, H. W.: *Children in Court.* New York, Public Affairs Committee, 1954.

183. Richman, Sol: Parent-Community Interaction as a Function of Adjustment of the Retarded Child, *American Journal of Mental Deficiency, 64:*556-560, November 1959.

184. Rinsland, Henry D.: *A Basic Vocabulary of Elementary School Children.* New York, Macmillan Company, 1945.

185. Rogers, Carl R.: *Counselling and Psychotherapy.* Boston, Houghton Mifflin Company, 1942.

186. Rogers, Dale Evans: *Angel Unaware.* Westwood, New Jersey, Fleming H. Revell Company, 1953.

187. Rosenquist, Lucy: *Young Children Learn to Use Arithmetic.* Boston, Ginn and Company, 1949.

188. Sarasan, Seymour B.: Mental Subnormality and the Behavioral Sciences, *Exceptional Children, 17:*243-247, May 1951.

189. Sarasan, Seymour B.: *Psychological Problems in Mental Deficiency,* rev. ed., New York, Harpers, 1953.

190. Schlesinger, E. R.: *Health Service for the Child.* New York, McGraw-Hill Book Company, 1953.

191. Schlotter, Bertha, and Svendsen, Margaret: *An Experiment in Recreation with the Mentally Retarded.* Springfield, Illinois, Department of Public Welfare, 1951.

192. Seaton, D. C.: *Physical Education Handbook,* 2nd ed., New York, Prentice-Hall, 1954.

193. Shirley, A. J.: *Handicraft in Metal.* Philadelphia, Lippincott, 1953.

194. Shotick, Andrew and Thate, Charles: Reactions of a Group of Educable Mentally Handicapped Children to a Program of Physical Education, *Exceptional Children, 26:*248-252, January 1960.

195. Smith, Marion Funk: *Teaching the Slow Learning Child.* New York, Harper & Brothers, 1954.

196. Stevens, Harvey A. and Szymanski, Gilbert: Planning a Training and Rehabilitation Building for Mentally Retarded Children, *Exceptional Children, 22:*229-232, March 1956.

197. Stinson, Ethelyn Lenore: *How to Teach Children Music.* New York, Harper & Brothers, 1941.

198. Stone, Clarence E.: *Progress in Primary Reading.* St. Louis, Webster Publishing Company, 1950.

199. Strang, Ruth: *Reporting to Parents,* 3rd ed., New York, Bureau of Publications, Teachers College, Columbia University, 1954.

200. Strauss, Alfred A., and Lehtinen, Laura E.: *Psychopathology and the Education of the Brain-Injured Child; Volume I, Fundamentals and Treatment.* New York, Grune and Stratton, 1947.

201. Strazzulla, Millicent: A Language Clinic for the Parents of Retarded Children, *American Journal of Mental Deficiency, 59:* 48-58, July 1954.

202. Strazzulla, Millicent: Nursery School Training for Retarded Children, *American Journal of Mental Deficiency, 61:*141-151, July 1956.

203. Strickland, Ruth G.: *How to Build a Unit of Work.* Washington, D. C., United States Government Printing Office, 1946.

204. Tashman, Harry F.: *Today's Neurotic Family, A Journey into Psychoanalysis.* New York, New York University Press, 1957. Shows how the parents' upbringing influences their children's lives.

205. Thorne, Gareth D.: Sex Education of Mentally Retarded Girls, *American Journal of Mental Deficiency, 62*:460-463, November 1957.

206. Thurston, Mildred W.: *Helping Children Live and Learn.* Washington, D. C., National Education Association, 1952.

207. Treat, Dorothy A., and Tate, Sally: *Nature Program Guide.* New York 28, National Audubon Society, 1000 Fifth Avenue, 1952.

208. Tredgold, Alfred F., and Tredgold, Roger Francis: *A Textbook of Mental Deficiency (Amentia),* 7th ed., Baltimore, Williams and Wilkins Company, 1952.

209. Tucker, Charlotte: *Betty Lee: A Mother's Story.* New York, Macmillan Company, 1954.

210. Tudyman, Al, and Groelle, M. C.: *A Functional Basic Word List for Special Pupils.* Pittsburgh 4, Stanwix House Incorporated, 1958.

211. Wallin, J. E. Wallace: *Education of Mentally Handicapped Children.* New York, Harper & Brothers, 1955.

212. Wanklemann, Willard: *Acts and Crafts for Elementary Teachers.* Dubuque, Iowa, W. C. Brown and Company, 1954.

213. Watkins, Harry L.: Visual Perception Training for the Moderately Retarded Child, *American Journal of Mental Deficiency, 61*:455-460, January 1957.

214. White, Robert W.: *The Abnorm*al Personality, 2nd ed., New York, Ronald Press, 1956.

215. Wolf, A. W. M.: *Helping Your Child's Emotional Growth.* Garden City, New York, Doubleday, 1954.

216. Wolk, Shirley Mae: A Survey of the Literature on Curriculum Practices for the Mentally Retarded, *American Journal of Mental Deficiency, 63*:826-839, March 1958.

217. Wood, Nancy E.: Causal Factors of Delayed Speech and Language Development, *American Journal of Mental Deficiency, 61*:706-708, April 1957.

218. The Woods School Yearbook. *The Pre-Adolescent Exceptional Child.* Langhorne, Pennsylvania, The Woods School, May 1953.

219. Wright, M. Erik, and Croley, High T.: *First Winfield Institute, Research on the Management of the Mentally Retarded Child.* Winfield, Kansas, Kansas State Training School, 1957.

220. Young, Milton A.: Academic Requirements of Jobs Held by Educable Mentally Retarded in the State of Connecticut, *American Journal of Mental Deficiency, 63*:792-802, March 1958.

221. Zudick, Leonard: A Conference Program with Parents of the Mentally Handicapped, *Exceptional Children, 21*:260-262, April 1955.

INDEX

A

Abacus, 171, 180-181
Ability
  assignments, 52
  to acquire habits, 11
  to be loyal, 11
  to observe, 30
  spread of, 16
Abstract terms, 9
Acceptance, 7-8
Action problems, 183
Activities
  a choice, 54
  adjustment, 4, 8
  addition, *see* Arithmetic
  drill, 34
  group, 54
  readiness, 30
  scaled, 52, 60
  training senses, 131
  types, 110
Aids, 41
Aim, 3
Alphabet, 27-28, 105
  charts, 103
Areas for lessons, 14
Arithmetic, 144-208
  abacus, 171, 180-181
  ability inventory, 148
  action problems, 183
  activities, 185-186
  add, 163
  addition, 177-179
    basic combinations, 182
    fractions, 197
    two-place, 187
  age
    CA, 146
    MA, 146
    readiness, 149-152
  auditory sense, 135, 157
  attention, 147
  basic skills, 146
  basis of program, 146
  bean bags, 171
  beginners' examples, 163
  borrowing, 187
  calendar, 200, 205-207
  carrying, 187
  check list, 149
  clock, 200-205
  computational skills, 183
  concept of
    one, 156
    two, 160
    three, 162
    ordinals, 161, 162, 166
  concrete material, 156
  counting
    by twos, 183
    by fives, 184
    by tens, 184
    devices, 147
  "crutches," 147
  days, 206
  demonstration, 199
  devices, 147, 181
  disabilities, 144
  division, 190
  domino pattern, 158, 170
  equation, 166-167, 177, 197
  examples, 163-165
  fewer, 186
  finger plays, 154-156
  first ordinal, 161
  flannel board, 168
  flash cards, 158, 170-171
  foot ruler, 192
  format for examples, 161-169, 172-179, 181, 189, 195-197

fractional parts, 194-196
fractions, 194-200
games, 171, 178, 182-193, 186
greater, 186
grouping, 156, 168-169, 178, 186
groups into fractions, 199
intermediate age span, 146
inventory of ability, 148
kinesthetic, 156
last, 162
length of drill, 147
less than, 165
linear measurement, 192
limitations
  of pupils, 144
  of workbooks, 148
materials, types, 149
matching, 170
meaningful numbers, 148
measurement, 192-194
methods, rote counting, 153
mental age check list, 149-152
mile, 193
money, 51-52, 191
motivation, 178
more than, 165
multiplication, 188
number
  place in series, 165
  6 through 10, 180
  rhymes, 154-156
objectives, 144
one-fourth, 200
one-half, 194
one and one, 161
one-third, 200
oral examples, 163
ordinals, 153, 161-162
parallel facts, 182
partial counting, 167-168, 178
pebbles as counters, 185
pound, 193
presentation, 198
procedure for beginners, 163-165
program, 145
progress chart, 149-152
pupils'
  attention span, 147
  disabilities, 144
readiness, 145-146, 160, 162
reading numbers, 188
relationship of numbers, 189-190
repetition, 148, 160, 176
research report, Committee of Seven, 148
retention, 168
rhymes, 154-156
ring toss, 171
Roman numerals, 207
rote counting, 153
second through tenth, 162, 166
semiconcrete material, 158
series, place numbers, 165
shapes, 192
shepherd's counting system, 184
subtraction, 172-176
  after addition, 160
  borrowing, 187
stencils, 160
symbol for one, 157
tactile aids, 158, 159
tallying by fives, 171
teaching
  concepts, 153
  materials, 149
  ordinals, 162
teens, 185
telephone, 182
thermometer, 84-86
temperature, 49, 84-86
tens to one hundred, 185-186
ten pins, 171
testing for readiness, 162
time, 200-206
two-place
  addition, 187
  subtraction, 187
tracing, 157, 159-160
visual
  aids, 158-159
  memory, 160
weeks, 206
weights, 193
width, 193
words—one, two, 171
workbooks, 148
written examples, 163
yard stick, 193
zero, 173, 175-176, 178, 183

Arousing interest, 178
Art, 113-126
  abilities, 113
  abstract, 114
  basis for program, 113
  clay, 62, 115-119, 126
  crayons, 125-126
  emotionally disturbed child, 115-120
  fancy, 9
  fanciful, 9
  free experiences, 123
  finger painting, 123
  frustration, 113-114
  grouping pupils, 114
  interest, 120
  imitative ability, 114
  instructing pupils, 119-120
  length of lesson, 120
  paints, 62
  presentation, 114
  procedure, 114, 120-121
  program, 113
  pupils' inexperience, 114
  purpose, 113
  relaxation, 62
  self-confidence, 115-119, 122
  types for EMH, 124
  weaving, 121
Assignment—reading, 40
Assimilating, 176
Association, 9
Attendance
  records, 46-48
  reports, 48
Attention, 8, 147
Audio-visual, 34, 127-135
  aids, 34
  field trips, 129-130
  films, 128-129
  materials, 127-135
  purpose, 127
  selection, 127
  sense training, 130-131
Auditory, 31
  ability, 31
  discrimination, 39
  perception, 31
  training, 31
  sense, 130, 157

B

Basic
  methods, 33-34
  skills, 14, 17, 20-24, 27, 33-34
Basis for programs, 3, 14-15, 26, 67
  arithmetic, 146
  art, 113
  audio-visual, 127
  language arts, 26
  reading, 29
  spelling, 104, 107
  writing, 93
Bean bags, 171
Behavior, 17, 63
Belongings, 10
Bibliography
  methods, 209-223
  unit, 78-84
Boundaries, 10
Brain-injured, 61-62, 109
Building a unit, 17
Bulletin board, 136-138
  arithmetic, 180
  arrangement, 136
  community, 16
  covered wagons, 137
  crafts, 128
  displays, 136-137
  flags, 128
  health, 14, 100
  lettering, 137
  materials, 135, 138
  pictures, 136
  post office, 35
  selection, 136
  social studies, 60
  sociogram, 140
  "Summer Fun," a unit, 88
  tactile aids, 158
  "The Air," charts, 90
  titles, 136-137
  visual aids, 158
  "Weather," charts, unit, 84-92
  writing, 94, 96

C

Cards
  flash, 34
  games, 36

Chalkboard, 33, 35, 97
Characteristics, 7-11
Charts, 33-34, 60, 68, 84, 90, 103, 142
Check list, 42
Child's
  contribution, 138
  progress, 65
  speech, 105
Choice of activity, 54
Choral readings, 49, 154-156
Civic responsibility, 5, 58
Classroom teacher in art, 121
Clay, 115-119
  modeling, 115-119
  pan, 100
  tracing, 99
"Clouds," a unit, 89
Committee of Seven, report, 148
Communication, 104
Community, 16
Comparisons, 133
Compensation, 6
Competence, socially, 55
Comprehension
  directions, 40
  exercises, 40
  sentences, 40
  words, 41
Concepts, 9, 28
Conferences, 64
Confidence, self-, 39, 115
Confusion
  letters, 39
  words, 39
Consonants, 102, 105
Control, 63
Coordination, 31
Correct habits, 4, 11, 44-45, 93
Counseling with parents, 63
Crafts, 53, 121-122
Criticism, 9
Curriculum, 12-33
  activities, 30
  complete experience, 33
  content, 14, 32
  core, 15, 26
  grouping, 12-13
  interpretation, 5
  language arts, 26
  mental age, 12, 28
  methods, 29
  motivation, 29
  oral language, 26
  place, 15
  plan, 20
  purpose, 15
  readiness, 28
  reading, 28
  scope, 14
  written language, 27
Cursive writing, 94

D

Daily lesson plan, 20, 86-92
Dance
  folk, 111
  Tinikling, 111-112
Defects, speech, 39
Delinquency, 4, 8, 10
Desk practice, writing, 98
Details, 17
Developing
  observation, 30
  coordination, 31
  perception, 31
  rhythm, 31
Devices, 51
Differences, 133-134
Difficulty
  between pupils, 63
  knowing right from wrong, 10
  recognizing boundaries, 10
Disappointments, 14
Discipline, 49, 62-63
  control of group, 62-63
  need for, 49, 62, 64
  new group, 62
  pupils' difficulties, 63
  remedies, 49, 62
  right and wrong, 10, 63
  trouble symptoms, 62
Discussion, 38
Discrimination
  auditory, 31, 39
  right from wrong, 10, 63
  visual, 30, 37-39

Displays
  bulletin board, 136
  change, 137
  mounted, 138
Dissimilar words and letters, 38
Distance, 193
Directions
  giving, 53
  to follow, 40, 63
Domino pattern, 132, 158, 170
Dramatization, 18, 26
Drill, 17
  activities, 34-36
  fire, 43
  words, 34

E

Economic efficiency, 4, 56
Educable mentally retarded
  characteristics, 7-11
  definition, 7
  eligibility to program, 12
  mental health, 5
  objectives, 4
  physical health, 5
  purpose of program, 3
  their future, 11
Education Policies Commission, 4
Emotional health, 5
Endings, s, ed, ing, 103
Enthusiasm of teacher, 29
Equation form, 166-167, 177, 197
Evaluate effort, 9
Evaluation of
  child, 65
  sociogram, 142
  unit, 24
Exercises for comprehension, 40
Experience
  charts, 27, 33-34, 60, 68, 84, 90
  stories, 33
  first-hand, 51-52
  to stimulate, 59
  unfavorable for brain-injured, 61-62
Explanation of unit, 20

F

Fanciful, 9
Fancy, 9
Fewer, 186
Field trip, 129
Films, 128
Finger painting, 120-122
Finger plays, 49, 154-156
Fire drill, 43-44
First day of school, 41-43
First-hand experience, 51
Flannel board, 168
Flash cards, 33-34, 41, 77, 158, 170-171
Followers, 9, 63
Foot ruler, 192
Format for examples, 161-169, 172-179, 181, 187, 189, 195-197
Four general objectives, 4
Fractions, 190-200
Frustration, 4, 7, 10, 29, 52, 58-59, 109, 113-114, 130, 147, 163
Future for EMH, 11

G

General
  experiences, 33-61
  objectives, 3-5
  seat activities, 51
Greater, 186
Grocery store, 50
Groups, 12-13

H

Habits, 4, 11, 13, 44-45, 48, 54, 93
Handicaps, multiple, 13
Health, 5, 14
Help promptly, 35
High school, 13
History, 18-19
Human relationships, 15, 68-69, 70-78, 84-89, 91-92
Humor, 11

I

Imagination, 9
Individual reading, 40
Initiative, 9
Instruction in art, 119-121
Integration
  of areas, 15, 26, 69, 84
  arithmetic, 75, 85, 89
  art, 76-77, 90

basic skills, 21, 23-24
health, 70, 85
homemaking, 70-71
Industrial arts, 76
language arts, 26, 71-73, 77, 85-89, 90-93
music, 74
nature study, 74
nutrition, 70, 85
physical education, 75
safety, 70, 85
science, 74, 84, 89
Interest, 4, 8, 10, 15, 18
Intermediate group, 12
Isolation, 62

J

Jigsaw puzzles, 38
Jokes, 11
Junior high school, 12
Judgment, 13

K

Kinesthetic, 101, 106, 122, 156

L

Labels, 41
Language arts, 26-27
Length, 193
Lesson
plans, 20
length, 103
Lettering, 136
Likeness, 133-134
Limited
attention span, 8
concepts, 9
imagination, 9
initiative, 9
interests, 10
reaction time, 8
sense of humor, 11
transfer, 8
vocabulary, 9
Love, 5, 8, 58-60
Loyalty, 11

M

Management
attention, 54
temperature, 49
ventilation, 49
Manuscript writing, 95-101
Markers for reading, 39
Matching games, 131-133
Materials, 16, 22, 24, 106
Maturation, 10
Measurement, 192-194
Mental
age, 28, 107
health, 5
Methods
examples, 163-165
basic skills, 33-35
fire drill, 44
readiness, 29-30
teaching a unit, 33
writing, 95-102
Mile, 193
Modified core curriculum, 15, 19-32, 67-92
Money, 51-52, 191
Monitors' duties, 46-48
More than, 165
Motivation, 15, 20, 22, 29, 94, 104
Multiple handicaps, 13
Muscular activity, 156
Music, 109-112
activities, 110
attention, 109
basis for program, 108
brain-injured, 109
folk dance, 111
procedure, 110-111
program, 108
teaching songs, 110
Tinikling dance, 111-112
trained teachers, 109
rhythm band, 108

N

Name, writing it, 27, 93
Narrow interests, 10
Number rhymes, 154-156
Numbers, *see* Arithmetic

O

Objectives for
arithmetic, 144
art, 113
audio-visual, 127
EMH, 3-5
music, 108

spelling, 107
sociogram, 139
unit, 20
writing, 93
Observation, 10, 17
Opposites, 133
Oral language
in reading, 39
in a unit, 26
Ordinals, 153
Over-teach, 180

P

Parents, 63-65
Pebbles for counters, 185
Perception
auditory, 31, 135
visual, 30, 134
Personal recognition, 35
Personality growth, 5
Phonics, 132
Phrases, 33, 35
Physical
health, 4, 5, 54-60
maturation, 10
Place of core, 15
Plan for core, 19
Post office, 35
Pound, 193
Praise, 5, 9, 58-60
Preparation for first day, 42
Prepositions, 9, 53
Presentation of
alphabet, 105
arithmetic, 147-149, 153-207
art, 119
cursive writing, 93-95
dance, 111
essential words, 104
manuscript writing, 93-101
songs, 110
tracing technique, 106
unit, 17, 29, 33, 67
Previous experience, 100
Primary group, 12
Printing set, 38
Procedure for
core, 24
group activity, 54
choices, 54
sociogram, 139
Progress reports, 65
Pupils'
check sheet, 42
duties, 43, 45, 48
names, 43
Purpose of
program for EMH, 3-6
modified core, 15
unit, 20

Q

Questions, sociogram, 42

R

Range of interest, 10
Reaction time, 8
Readiness
arithmetic, 146
language arts, 27-30, 35
spelling, 106
subtraction, 160
writing, 93, 95
Reading
activities, 30
comprehension, 40
content, 29
core curriculum, 28
methods, 29
motivation, 29
new material, 29
oral, 39
readiness, 28-29
use of line markers, 39
Realization, self-, 4, 57
Recognition of boundaries, 10
Records
attendance, 45-47
days, 205
months, 205
pupils', 42
sociogram, 141-142
weather, 84
weeks, 205
Relationships, parent-teacher, 63, 65
Relaxation of pupils, 49, 62
Repetition, 34, 93, 107, 148, 160, 176
Reports to parents, 65

Responsibility, 5, 15, 48
Retention, 34, 39, 93, 107, 148, 160, 176
Rhymes, 154-156
Ring toss, 171
Room duty, 45, 49
Routine tasks, 45, 48-49
Ruler, 38
Rules, 43, 49, 51

S

Safety, 14
Schedule, 42, 45
Scrap books, 132
Seating, 45-47
Self-realization, 4, 57
Self-confidence, 4, 93
Self-preservation, 5, 34
Sensitivity, 7
Sentences, 33, 84
Sensory training, 127, 130-137
Shapes, 192
Shepherd's counters, 184
Short attention span, 8
Sight vocabulary, 105
Slow reaction time, 8
Social
  acceptance, 4
  adjustment, 4
  competence, 4, 55-56
  experience, 14
  studies, 60
  status, 93
Sociogram, 139-144
  charting, 142
  evaluating, 142
  graphs, 140-141
  procedure, 139
  purpose, 139
  questions, 142
  recording, 142
  utilizing, 143
Speech
  defects, 39
  difficulties, 105
Spelling, 104-108
  alphabet, 105
  communication, 104
  essential words, 104
  formal, 106
  importance of, 107
  kinesthetic sense, 106
  mental age, 107
  motivation, 104
  readiness, 106
  tactile sense, 106
  tracing, 106
  vowels, 105
Stencils, 160
Subjects for units, 16, 18-19
Supplies, 41
Squared paper, 38-39, 96, 192

T

Tachistoscope, 36
Tactile, 122, 157
Teacher
  accepting, 60
  characteristics, 61
  counseling, 63-64
  enthusiasm, 29
  importance of, 60-61
  interest, 29
  parent relationships, 63
  traditional, 60
  responsibility, 3, 44-45, 48
Teaching
  comparisons, 133
  cultural heritage, 3
  differences, 133-134
  historical heritage, 3
  likenesses, 133-134
  opposites, 133
  techniques, 33
  tracing, 106
Temperature, 49, 84-86
Ten pins, 171
Thermometer, 84-86
Tic-tac-toe, 35
Transfer of learning, 8

U

Unit, 15, 17, 33, 67-93
  activities, 30-31, 34, 67-92
  alphabet, 27-28
  arithmetic, 73, 85
  art, 76
  basic skills, 17, 71-73
  bibliography, 26, 78-84

"Clouds," a unit, 89-93
complete experience, 33
content, 22
coordination, 31
core, 15
definition, 17
detailed explanations, 17
development, 70, 72-76
evaluation, 25, 77-78, 92
experience charts, 27, 33-34
explanation, 20
flash cards, 33-34, 41, 77, 158
health, 70, 85
industrial arts, 76
integration, 26, 69, 85, 89, 104
language arts, 26, 71-72, 85
lesson plans, 20, 86-92
methods, 29, 33-34, 67-77, 85
motivation, 20, 29, 67-93
music, 74
nature study, 74
objectives, 20, 60, 84, 89
observation, 30
outline, 19-20
physical education, 75
phrases, 83
plan, 33
procedure, 18, 24, 77, 86-92
purpose, 20, 67, 84, 89
readiness, 27-28
rhythm, 31
safety, 70, 85
sample units, 67-93
science, 74, 84, 89
sentences, 33-35
sight vocabulary, 27, 35
subjects, 16, 18-20, 67
"Summer Fun," a unit, 67-84
"The Weather," a unit, 84-89
types, 17

V

Visual
development, 30
discrimination, 37-39, 134
observation, 30
Vocabulary, 10, 27, 34-35, 41, 53
labels, 41
sight, 27, 34, 104
survival, 34
Vocational placement, 13, 51, 66
Vowels, 105

W

Wall chart, 33
Weaving, 121
Width, 193
Word
activities, 34-36
drill, 34-36
games, 35-36
recognition, 41
wheel, 35
window, 36
Words
dissimilar, 38
for self-preservation, 34
frequently used, 104
similar, 38
Worksheet, 21-26, 77, 161-167, 169, 172-177, 179, 187, 189, 195-197, 201-205
Writing, 93-104
alphabet charts, 103
chalkboard, 97
clay, 99-100
consonants, 102
cursive, 94-95
habits, 93
kinesthetic, 101
length of lesson, 103
manuscript, 94-99, 100, 102
muscular control, 93, 95
objectives, 93
practice, 98
presentation, 97, 101
position, 95-96
procedures, 98, 102
proficiency of teacher, 95
readiness, 93, 95
spacing, 94, 97
tracing, 95, 99-100
value of writing, 93

Y

Yard stick, 193

Z

Zero, *see* Arithmetic